5.00

D1067783

English Villages

by the same author

SCOTTISH BORDER COUNTRY

1 (*overleaf*) *Geddington, Northamptonshire*

ENGLISH VILLAGES

F. R. Banks

Photographs by Edwin Smith

B. T. BATSFORD LTD

London

To my Wife

First published 1963

© F. R. Banks, 1963

MADE AND PRINTED IN GREAT BRITAIN BY
WILLIAM CLOWES AND SONS LTD, LONDON AND BECCLES
FOR THE PUBLISHERS B.T.BATSFORD LTD
4 FITZHARDINGE STREET, PORTMAN SQUARE, LONDON W.I

CONTENTS

7

ACKNOWLEDGMENT

I SHOULD like to say 'thank you' to Mr Edwin Smith for his excellent selection of photographs of English Villages by which the value of this book is enhanced, if indeed it is not largely dependent on them. The Publishers, wisely, I think, did not insist that Mr Smith should attempt to provide illustrations for exactly those villages I have mentioned, but have allowed him to follow his own course, sometimes coinciding, sometimes parallel, through the regions of England.

I should like to acknowledge the debt I owe to Dr W. G. Hoskins, the author, and Messrs Hodder & Stoughton, the publishers, for the help I received from *The Making of the English Landscape*. I should also like to record my thanks to Mr Alec Clifton-Taylor for the assistance I obtained from his book, *The Pattern of English Building*, and to Mr Samuel Carr, of Messrs B. T. Batsford, for his great kindness and encouragement.

F. R. BANKS

LIST OF ILLUSTRATIONS

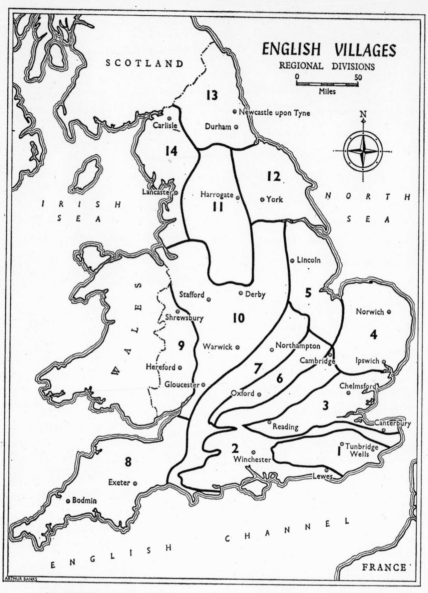

ENGLISH VILLAGES
REGIONAL DIVISIONS

1 The Weald and Greensand
   Country
2 The Chalk Country
3 The Clay Country
4 East Anglia
5 The Fens and Lincolnshire
6 Between the Chalk and the
   Limestone
7 The Limestone Country
8 South-West England
9 The Western Marches
10 The Midland Plain
11 The Pennines
12 East of the Pennines
13 North-East England
14 North-West England

Preamble

ONE OF the problems facing the author setting out to write a book on English Villages is deciding whether to generalise or particularise—I mean whether to arrange the villages in groups and describe them broadly as types, according say to their building materials or the kind of country in which they are situated, or whether to try to deal with them individually, irrespective of any features they may have in common, in the belief that every village has its own unique personality.

The disadvantage of the second method in a book of this nature is that it is impossible to mention even a fair proportion of all the attractive or historic villages in England; the value of the first is that only in this way can we hope to reduce the infinite diversity of our villages to some sort of order. The advantages then are in favour of the first method. One thing I could be sure about, however, if I adopted this method: as soon as I had 'typed' *your* particular village, you would protest it was not like that at all. It has, you would say, its own special features, the result it may be of its unusual setting, dependent on some local variation in geology, or of its history: one of the Conqueror's followers decided to build a castle here or some country industry became established in the village. A main road perhaps runs through the village or, even more significantly, avoids it, with the result that it was able to develop its pattern of life independently of the world outside, as so many villages seem to have done.

I decided therefore on a combination of both methods. But first I have tried to describe briefly how the English village has grown up. I have attempted, however superficially, to find the reasons why our villages have developed in the particular way they have and why they appear today in the form and pattern that is familiar to us. Every village has certain basic features which it shares with others. Whatever the differences between one village and the next, all villages have something of a common historical and sociological background.

The next problem to solve was how to collect the villages into groups or divide them into regions. I decided at the outset to ignore the county boundaries: these seem to me in most cases to be artificial divisions bearing very little relation to the geology or physical geography of the landscape. Division according to geographical regions—the North, the Midlands, and so on—would be altogether too vague, and hardly any improvement on division by counties. (I shall have something to say later about the treatment usually accorded to the North.) Much the best method of dividing the country appeared to be one based on the geological structure, and this is the one I have adopted, with some local modifications which I have set out at the beginning of the regional survey.

One of the things that impresses itself on any traveller through the English countryside is that, in spite of the similarity in the general development of almost every village, and despite all the efforts to impose a dull uniformity on our landscape by the mass producers of the nineteenth and twentieth centuries, there still remains a wealth of difference between the villages of one part of the country and another. Nothing is more evident than the change in style and feeling from the limestone villages of the Cotswolds to the timber-framed villages of East Anglia or the Welsh marches, the brick and timber villages of the Weald, the cob and thatch villages of much of Devon and west Somerset and the gritstone villages of the Pennines.

The most fundamental difference between the villages in one region of England and another is indeed their building materials, and this variation depends to a great extent on the geological structure that underlies them; the bones beneath the skin that not only mould the landscape but provide most of the material for the village buildings. Before the railways came to transport cheap slates from Wales or dump down wagon-loads of bricks in country that possessed good stone quarries, the village builder was obliged to use the natural materials which his own district afforded. This is in truth the great secret underlying the beauty of our villages. Nature's productions harmonise best with the landscape in the regions where they are produced; alien buildings and materials always lead to an unsatisfactory appearance.

One of the great charms of English villages, I need hardly stress, is their infinite variety. You can divide them according to regions, counties, building materials or any other method you please, and whichever way you look at them, no two villages are exactly the same. Each village possesses its own individuality—its own personality, if you like—the result of its particular setting, its history and traditional style and the part played in modifying these by local craftsmen, their names unrecorded. Traditions are handed down from father to son; sometimes they are spread abroad in the countryside and show themselves in several villages in a particular district. But even where the villages in any region seem to follow the same pattern and use the same materials, the church, the manor house, the farm buildings and the cottages will vary from one village to the next. No two churches are exactly the same, no two groups of cottages exactly alike. Generalising about villages is the most dangerous thing to do.

To decide which villages to describe in my regional survey was a major problem. There are 13,000 villages in England, it has been estimated, so the chance of my leaving out a large proportion of your favourites (unless they happen to be general favourites) is pretty high. I decided, because of the scope and size of the book, to limit the number of villages to 300, and to spread them over the country as evenly as possible, always keeping in mind that nature or history has ordained that some regions shall be rich in beautiful or well-built villages, by reason of their situation or building materials, the development of agriculture or the growth of some industry, such as the great wool trade, while others will suffer from the lack of some if not all of these factors.

The decision, too, whether some places were large villages or small towns was difficult to make. I first intended to exclude every place that had (or once had) a market, as this indicated that it could be regarded as the nucleus of its district and hence rather more than a self-contained, independent village. But in medieval and Tudor times, at least, many villages had regular markets without becoming agricultural centres on any wide scale or (as in the Cotswolds and East Anglia) more than limited centres of rural industry. Many places without markets have expanded into towns, because of the vagaries of the railway system, for instance, or the growth of new industries, while other places that were once important market towns have decayed (if indeed that is a happy term) and are now no more than loose villages.

In consequence, I gave up the struggle and decided, perhaps rather arbitrarily, to exclude all the places that were spelt in capital letters on the Ordnance Survey $\frac{1}{4}$-inch-to-the-mile map and were presumably regarded by this government department as towns. This meant that I had, very sadly, to leave out such places as Tenterden and Cranbrook, Lavenham and Kimbolton, Burford and Chipping Campden, Dunster and Chagford, Henley-in-Arden and others which I would dearly have loved to include. But when I came to Haworth and Hawkshead, I revolted against this self-imposed dictatorship—these, I declare, are genuine villages and I could not leave them out at any price. I decided finally to rely on my own judgement about what constituted a town, and as a result some 'capital-letter' village/towns—Lavenham, Burford and Dunster, for example—found their way back again.

I have tried as far as possible to concentrate on the villages themselves—their settings and structure—in my regional survey. In describing the regions, I have kept the geology as simple as possible: in some parts of England the geological pattern is extremely complex, but I have tried not to involve myself in too much detail, except where this bears directly on the subject of villages. In my descriptions, all necessarily brief, of the individual villages, I have often made no mention of that centre of the village community, the parish church, however interesting it may be, especially where it forms no integral part of the village scene. For this reason, too, I may have said nothing about many an interesting and much-visited building if it happens to lie outside the village. At Burwash in Sussex, for instance, I have not mentioned Bateman's, the charming home of Rudyard Kipling; it is a good half-mile from the village and forms no part of it. I have said practically nothing about the insides of the houses and churches, except where they may have some influence on the outward pattern and style of the village. Finally, you will find precious little about village life—the kernel of which the buildings are merely the shell—in these pages. My purpose in fact, for those who like definitions, is topographical, not sociological.

I have been visiting these villages over a good many years, and if changes that would affect my judgement have taken place in any of them within the last year or two, I am indeed very sorry. I have revisited as many villages as I could get to for the benefit of this book: it would have been nice to have seen them all again, but this was not possible. If I manage to entice you out of your way to visit one of these villages only to discover that a hideous bungalow suburb or caravan city has been created outside it or an ugly new power-station has been built overshadowing it—as has happened to an ancient and charming village not ten miles from where I live—then I crave your indulgence, and hope you will tell me about it.

The Growth of the English Village

IF A visitor from Mars, well versed in World geography, were to land in almost any part of England, he would know which country he had arrived in, I suggest, by the pattern of hedged or walled fields, with villages dotted about at more or less regular intervals. Nothing, indeed, distinguishes the English scene from the Continental so much as this patchwork of fields, green, brown or yellow, according to the season or the state of agriculture, divided by hedgerows or dry-stone walls, with here and there the brick, stone or timber-framed dwellings of a village forming the nucleus of a small but compact area.

Though this pattern of course extends into Scotland and Wales— and on the other hand is less obvious in the moorland districts of the north and west—it is the essential part of most of the English scene. Villages of varying size and character are to be found all over England: it has been computed, as I said in the Preamble, that there are more than 13,000 of them. And this figure takes no account of hamlets, which are not merely smaller versions of villages but have a different origin, as I hope to show.

The surprising thing is that although the pattern of English fields has taken the form it has now only since the eighteenth century (in most parts of the country, at any rate), the majority of our villages have occupied their sites since Anglo-Saxon times. It can almost be said that they are the one unchanging feature in the landscape, at least as far as the human effect on it is concerned. But we are so familiar with the idea of the village as the basis of our rural society that we take it for granted; we fail to appreciate that England, more than any other country, is essentially a land of villages.

Of all the forms of ancient settlement, the village as we know it in England is only one, but it is the one that has survived most successfully. As I say, it can be met with in every part of England, though naturally, for historical or economic reasons, villages are more common and clustered closer together in some parts of the country than in others. In the upland regions of the north and west, too, the map shows a mixed pattern of villages, hamlets and isolated farmsteads, all of some antiquity, but in the midland and eastern counties the village is the commonest (and in some parts, almost the only) form of settlement.

It can be said with confidence, then, that the village community is the basic unit of settlement in the English countryside. In spite of all the inconveniences of its structure, the form of village introduced by the Anglo-Saxons was a remarkable foundation, not only because it repeated itself over the greater part of England, but also because it survived practically untouched for over a thousand years, and has persisted in its essential features until the present day. How far it will survive unmodified in the future is a matter for conjecture which is outside the scope of this book.

The village as conceived by the Anglo-Saxons was more than a collection of farms and holdings; it was a systematic expression of a definite way of life, based on the need to centralise agricultural activity in one particular place. The inhabitants of this cluster of houses, standing in the centre of its fields—the centre of its world, in fact—were involved in an intricate series of problems which necessitated continual co-operation between them. Agreement had to be reached on the methods of cultivation and the division of the agricultural year, so that these could be planned to the advantage of all the villagers.

The Anglo-Saxon Settlement

England became a land of villages during the settlement of the Angles and Saxons from the fifth century onwards, and a large proportion of our villages were in existence by the time of the Norman invasion of 1066. If this sounds surprising, it may be because it is not generally realised that the Anglo-Saxon settlement extended over more than six centuries, or 20 generations—longer than the time from the accession of the first Tudor to the present day. It should be remembered also that when the Anglo-Saxons began to arrive there were to all intents no fields, precious little agriculture and no villages. The settlement was essentially a great pioneering venture by an agricultural people. To appreciate the difficulties that were involved, we must look at the country as it was then through the eyes of an immensely practical immigrant farmer.

From about the middle of the fifth century onwards, villages were slowly but steadily established in England by one northern European tribe after another. The Jutes from what is now Denmark invaded and settled in Kent and the Isle of Wight; the Saxons from North Germany settled in Essex, Middlesex, Surrey, Sussex and other southern regions, from which they pushed out westward; and their neighbours the Angles set foot in Norfolk and Suffolk, from which they expanded northward as far as the Scottish border. By the middle of the seventh century the greater part of the country had been divided among the three kingdoms of Northumbria, Mercia and Wessex, and the work of colonisation could go forward more rapidly.

Not only were the Anglo-Saxons a gregarious people by nature, but the open-field system which they introduced necessitated their living together in close settlements. Through the use of iron implements unknown to their forerunners, the Romano-British inhabitants of these islands, they were able to clear many of the thick forests that covered much of the country and to farm the rich soils of the valleys and lowlands. Here they built their villages, in contrast with the existing British hamlets mostly situated on the hills.

Much of the English landscape could be seen to be divided into three kinds of country after the Anglo-Saxon system of agriculture had become established: the arable land, the open meadow and pastureland, and the unreclaimed forest, fen and moorland. Of these, the arable land was the most conspicuous and important; here tillage was carried on in large unenclosed fields or plots, subdivided into long narrow strips. Each farmer cultivated a number of strips, scattered about in various places, not kept together in a compact allotment, and each strip was separated from his neighbour's by unsown furrows or fringes of uncultivated grass. This intermixing of strips meant that the methods of cultivation concerned not only the individual farmer but the village community as a whole. When the crops had been harvested, the village cattle, communally owned, were allowed to graze over the stubble of the whole range of fields.

2 *Ashwell, Hertfordshire*

The open-field system was not the only one that existed in Anglo-Saxon England. In the north and the south-west, in particular, considerable tracts of land were reclaimed wholesale by the efforts of individuals or small groups of settlers, living in isolated farmsteads or hamlets. But over most of the southern and eastern regions—say, at least three-quarters of the country—from Dorset to Durham and from Norfolk to the Welsh border, the pattern of open fields provided the unvarying scene.

It used to be thought that a distinction could be made between the smaller settlements—hamlets and farmsteads—scattered over the north and west of England, where the so-called Celtic way of life, it was believed, had continued unhampered, and the compact 'nucleated' villages (as they are called) of the midlands, east and south. In these regions, it was argued, the Angles and Saxons had destroyed everything in their path and subsequently built new villages on new sites. Certainly, the Anglo-Saxons seem to have avoided the old sites (a point I will come back to in a moment) and their villages were more concentrated than those of the native Britons they displaced; and in the south and east the tendency was towards nucleated villages, while in the north and west it was towards scattered hamlets. But in the south-west counties, for instance, where hamlets and single farmsteads are to be met with everywhere, large compact villages were also in existence before the Norman Conquest. At the same time, though villages predominated in the midlands and the eastern counties, hamlets and farmsteads, too, were enjoying a healthy existence before the Normans came.

The establishment of the English village on the plan we recognise, it cannot be stressed too often, is directly related to the open-field system which was the outstanding contribution of the Anglo-Saxons. If it was the foundation of the village as such that determined the pattern of the fields, it was the system of agriculture that decided the general plan of the village.

This system, as I say, was to be found practically all over England before the Norman Conquest. Because of the lack of evidence for open fields in some of the outlying counties of England—Devon and Cornwall, for instance, Lancashire and the north-west—it used to be contended that the Anglo-Saxons had never brought these regions under their control. But Braunton, in Devon, is one place where the

3 *Little Barrington, Gloucestershire*
4 *Chiselborough, Somerset*

open fields have survived almost untouched, and the land is still cultivated very much as it was in Saxon times. It seems likely, indeed, that the open field was established as the basis of agriculture all over these regions, but that it had disappeared—as it is known to have done in Kent and Essex—before the first enclosures into hedged fields were made, by the Tudors, and long before any maps were drawn to prove whether or not they were in existence.

Romano-British Survivals

The village, considered as a collection of family habitations, was not of course an invention of the Anglo-Saxons. Though the Romans themselves congregated in towns or retired to villa-farmsteads, many settlements of the native Britons were to be found in England during the Roman period. But the Britons, not tied to a complicated field system as the Saxons were, preferred to scatter themselves over the countryside in small family groups, leaving a piece of land when they had exhausted its possibilities for cultivation, and moving on to the next. It seems likely that most of the more permanent settlements were already being deserted in the fourth century, when the influence of Rome began to wane, and it is not known whether any villages in England have actually been inhabited from Romano-British times onward, though future excavation may of course prove this.

All settlements depend on the natural physical conditions for their origin. In prehistoric and pre-Saxon times, the low-lying lands were covered with forest or scrub or made impassable by marsh, and the settlements consequently tended to be on the hill-tops and ridges, which were dry, accessible and more easily defended, or on the banks of navigable rivers. The Anglo-Saxons cleared the woodlands and cultivated the valleys, and hence were able to plant their villages on new sites which had not been practicable in the previous era.

High-lying villages on the kind of site favoured by the Britons may well prove a fruitful source of excavation, particularly where they are surrounded by other evidence in the shape of British cemeteries and the like. One thing we cannot be sure of, in the present state of our knowledge, is how far any existing settlement may have affected the plan of the village. The late O. G. S. Crawford, in *Archaeology in the Field*, declared that when the Angles and Saxons settled in the valleys, they left many of the upland areas untouched, and life in the surviving Romano-British villages went on unmolested. Where the uplands between the valleys were narrow ridges, the new villages in the valleys on either hand marked out a common boundary along the intervening ridge and the older British villages tended to get squeezed out. But where the valleys were farther apart and the upland areas too remote, the ancient village survived.

As an example of such a survival, Dr W. G. Hoskins, in his penetrating book, *The Making of the English Landscape*, mentions Ashmore, standing high up on the edge of Cranborne Chase, on the borders of Dorset and Wiltshire. Though the village has a Saxon name, it has probably, he thinks, been lived in continuously since Romano-British times. Not only does it stand on a hill-top, in country that is thickly strewn with the evidence of early man, including several Romano-British villages, but it is built round a large embanked pond that gives the village its name of 'Ash-mere', the 'pond of the ash-tree'. O. G. S. Crawford has said that some of these embanked ponds date at least from the beginning of the Christian era and that upland villages taking their names from such ponds 'have either been continuously occupied since pre-Saxon times, or . . . were re-occupied, after abandonment for a period, by early Saxon settlers'. Another clue to the early origin of this village is that the parish church is situated on the outskirts, at some distance from the pond, as might be expected if it is of much later foundation.

If all this supposition is true, the origin of Ashmore is evidence that we cannot take its existing name to prove the antiquity or otherwise of a village. It is obvious that the names of most villages must have been given not by the inhabitants themselves but by their neighbours. Your village to you and your fellow-villagers is simply 'the village'; it is the people of the neighbouring villages who first called it Norton or Sutton or whatever, to distinguish it from their own and other villages. In the same way, the Saxon name was conceivably given to Ashmore by the 'new' English settlers living in the valley.

The Anglo-Saxon Village

Though the Angles and Saxons covered practically all England with their villages, these were, by the nature of the terrain and the progress of colonisation, rather more common in some regions than in others. In the east Midlands and East Anglia, among the earliest regions to be settled, villages were established on the average only about two or three miles apart, even allowing for the fact that the later Scandinavian settlement accentuated the congestion. But in west Devon and Cornwall, going towards the other extreme, they were half a dozen miles or more apart, though this is probably because many of the hamlets and farmsteads established during the Romano-British era were still in existence here.

Unlike those of their British forerunners, the sites which the Anglo-Saxons selected for their settlements were determined basically by economic considerations (not by those of defence or accessibility) and they built their villages where the economic needs were most easily satisfied. As their implements and their methods of farming improved, the forest was cleared more quickly and the marshlands were drained, and cultivation spread up the valleys and over the lowlands. In consequence, the Anglo-Saxons built many of their villages in the river valleys or near springs below the hills, where they had better shelter and a plentiful supply of water, as well as deeper and richer soil. Some at least of the Anglo-Saxon village names betray a topographical origin, revealing their reliance on natural features.

The Anglo-Saxons, it must be stressed, were fundamentally a farming population; they were no town dwellers, and they avoided the Roman walled towns, as far as these had survived. When they had secured for themselves good farm lands, their greatest desire was to build a village and till the soil on the open-field system of agriculture. The sites which the Saxons chose, though not necessarily the best positioned, have mostly remained to this day. Where peaceful populations have settled and struck root over the centuries, they are not easily transplanted. When the various communities had staked out and begun cultivating their share of land, custom and ownership consolidated the choice.

The work of colonisation begun following the first Anglo-Saxon invasions was carried on steadily from generation to generation. Some of the villages were founded as early as the fifth century, as can be seen from the evidence of their place-names or from that unearthed by archaeologists from heathen cemeteries. Others are recorded for the first time in charters, increasing in number from the seventh to the tenth century. As Sir Frank Stenton says in his fascinating *Anglo-Saxon England*, charters prove by the middle of the tenth century 'the existence of innumerable villages, each known by a permanent name and maintained by a territory of which the boundaries could be described in minute detail'.

Every village, of course, has experienced some changes in plan since its foundation, and it is usually difficult to distinguish the original pattern beneath the later accretions. Here and there, however, it is just possible to find some village that bears visible evidence of its Anglo-Saxon origins. An outstanding example of such a village is Laxton, in Nottinghamshire, where in fact we can see the very rare survival of the open-field system. Named 'Laxintune' in *Domesday Book*—the 'tun' (township or village) of Leaxa's people—it still consists almost entirely of a group of some eight or ten farmsteads, with the church in the middle, completely surrounded by its three large fields, marked on the Ordnance Survey map as West Field, Mill Field and South Field. These are still divided into the tenant farmers' holdings and cultivated on the old three-course rotation system evolved by the Anglo-Saxons.

The only significant change at Laxton is in the farmsteads themselves. In Saxon times the buildings would have been made entirely of wood—the walls of split trunks of trees set vertically, side by side, and the roof, too, completely of timber, of which there was plenty to spare. (It was only when timber began to become scarce that houses started to be made with a wooden framework filled in with other material.) I have mentioned Braunton in Devon as another village where the open-field system can still be seen; yet another place in which the Anglo-Saxon method of cultivation has survived is the Isle of Axholme (Lincolnshire), where the village of Haxey still stands in the centre of its open fields. In other places it is possible to trace the Anglo-Saxon bones beneath the more recent flesh; the small village of Bygrave, near Baldock (Hertfordshire), for example, lost its open fields only within living memory.

I must stress again that although the village surrounded by its open fields is associated inseparably with the Anglo-Saxon settlement, it was not in fact the only kind of settlement, even in those times. As Sir Frank Stenton has pointed out, 'No single type of settlement can ever have prevailed throughout the whole, even of southern England. On heavy lands, and, indeed, wherever there was a prospect of a steady return to co-operative agriculture, coerls tended to live together in villages. But as late as the eighth century life for perhaps a quarter of the English people was a struggle for existence against unprofitable soil and a scrubland vegetation which would spread again over uncultivated fields on any slackening of effort. It was by individual enterprise that these poor lands had been brought into cultivation, and innumerable isolated farmsteads bearing Anglo-Saxon names remain as memorials of the process.'

In the hillier country of the north and west of England, the village community centred in its open fields was indeed less common. These were regions given over principally to stock raising and the characteristic unit of settlement was the hamlet or isolated farmstead. The co-operation and communal services demanded by the open-field village were not required here. Habitations were few and far between: 'the houses which lie on the boundary of the parish are scattered about in small clusters; here two or three, there three or four. These clusters often have names of their own, and it seems a mere chance that the name borne by one of them should also be the name of the whole parish.'

The Basic Types of Village

For all the apparently infinite variety among those English villages whose plan has not been obscured by the uncontrolled rash of building in the nineteenth and twentieth centuries, nearly all villages of early origin fall into one or other of three basic groups. After taking account of topographical limitations, it will be found that the Anglo-Saxon village was usually either (1) built along a single street (or sometimes two streets at right angles), or (2) grouped round a central green or square, or (3) merely a haphazard conglomeration of houses scattered about with no apparent nucleus and without any order or relation to each other. The last type may seem to include an indeterminate variety of possibilities, but villages of this kind can usually be shown to have had originally a common purpose.

Later changes in the plan, such as the filling up of the green or square with dwellings, may disguise the fact that the village belongs fundamentally to one of these types. Even the comparatively few 'planned' villages, chiefly of the eighteenth and nineteenth centuries

(Milton Abbas, in Dorset, is a well-known example), though built on—or transferred to—new sites, will usually be found to follow the ancient pattern. Only the nineteenth-century industrial villages (not the earlier ones) seem to conform to no plan.

Though popular conception paints the central green as the nucleus of any village in England, it is in fact confined largely to the eastern side of the country, and especially to the coastal counties from Northumberland to Essex. The reason for this regional limitation may be that it was on this side of the country where the Anglo-Saxon settlers felt themselves most vulnerable to attack. In the troubled country of the Scottish Border, for instance, defence was long the prime consideration, and here the square or 'green' village, as it is usually called, is the traditional type.

Villages, it would appear from this, were most likely built four-square round an open space or green, in the earlier days at least, because this was the best method of defence. The houses, built close together, formed in effect a wall round the perimeter, while the green was an enclosure into which the cattle could be driven in time of need. A somewhat similar defence system can perhaps be seen in the 'fortified' hill-top villages of Italy, where the outer walls of the dwellings are built end to end to make an unbroken rampart. A better example is the native village of central Africa, where the huts are arranged round the outside of a roughly circular pound into which the livestock are driven each night to protect them from predatory animals. The openings between adjacent huts are then sealed by thorn fences which the tribesman is expected to keep in good repair.

In the villages of Anglo-Saxon England, it seems, a similar plan was evolved to protect the inhabitants and their possessions from predators from across the sea (in the shape of fresh bands of settlers) or in the north from across the Border, or at least from the many wolves and other wild beasts that roamed the thickly forested country. Though the obligation to keep closed the entrances to the central space would lapse with the lessening fear of attackers and the dying out of the larger wild animals, the basic plan survived, though now roads were made leading into the square at every angle from the fields outside.

Rights on the village green were jealously guarded in most places and the only obstruction allowed on it was the communal well, the essential water supply without which the village could not have survived and which more often than not decided its actual site. No other permanent building was permitted on the green; even the church, especially if it is of Saxon or early medieval origin, stands to one side, though in the north the church-tower often played a significant part, even as far south as Yorkshire, as a look-out post and a refuge for the villagers against raiders from over the Border. Until recent times, as a general rule, the only buildings to be found on many a village green were the school and the smithy, both post-medieval institutions.

In some places, as I mentioned, the original plan of the village has been obscured by the fact that houses or other buildings have been erected on the green. Quite recently I read of a Worcestershire village where it was proposed to build a new housing estate on the green (a proposal heartily resented by the villagers, I am glad to say), but this sort of encroachment, though often represented as something villainously modern, has been going on for centuries. Many villages whose streets are arranged in the form of a compact square or rectangle (Lacock, in Wiltshire, is a famous example) may have originated as green villages, but the open space has been built over at an early date. Many greens, too, were split up during the Parliamentary enclosures of the eighteenth century, when there was no longer any practical necessity for them.

The second type of English village is the 'street', a type which in fact was more widely spread and more rudimentary than the green village. It is common sense that if you found a new community, you try to take the line of least resistance by building the houses along the sides of an existing thoroughfare (if not along the bank of a navigable waterway). If you want to extend or enlarge the village, you build further houses at either end, a process that has been carried to the ridiculous in the 'ribbon development' of modern times. Many street villages can be proved to be of great antiquity; Moreton-in-Marsh, in Gloucestershire, mentioned in A.D. 714, is only one of a number of villages built along the sides of Roman roads which have been brought into use again. More of the street villages, however, were built along thoroughfares constructed in Saxon or medieval times, and the church came to occupy a dominating position, often on a rise in the centre of the village or facing one end. Coxwold, in the North Riding, first recorded in A.D. 758, is an example of this.

Examples of the basic street plan can be recognised in innumerable villages all over the country. But in some villages the street is so wide that it is difficult to decide off-hand whether they are street or green villages. Until transport made it easier to congregate in the nearest town, many villages had weekly sales of cattle and chattels, and the width of the street was increased in time to accommodate these markets. To bring in Moreton-in-Marsh again; though the site of the village was obviously determined by the Roman road, the buildings are now set back behind wide strips of green, so the impression is more of a green village than a street village.

In both kinds of village, in fact, local variations are to be found everywhere, even between one village and the next. The 'street', for instance, though no more complicated than required by convenience, was far from being a mere repetitive string of houses lining the road. Our ancestors showed a natural feeling for landscape in the siting of the church and other buildings, the planting of trees and the separation of the dwellings from the road by broad green verges. The habits of settlement and cultivation, too, were modified by the peculiarities of local topography; a river, a marsh, a range of hills or a stretch of unreclaimed forest produced infinite variations from the basic plan.

The third type of village, that which is neither grouped round a square nor strung out along a street, may be thought to cover every other eventuality. The houses in these 'fragmented' villages, as they are called, seem to have been planted down singly or in small groups with no discernible plan and they are usually linked by a maze of crooked lanes and paths in no apparent order. It has been suggested that such villages mostly originated as clearances in wooded country, though some of them are certainly the product of squatters on common pastureland or waste land, as has happened, for instance, on the commons of Surrey and Hampshire in comparatively recent times.

The older of the fragmented villages were developed as further clearances were made in the great forests which covered much of England in Saxon times. There was no agreed plan, presumably, and houses were built by individual settlers as space was cleared. Though they kept together as a roughly-knit family rather than acting as individuals building their own separate farmsteads, these settlers were in the nature of explorers, not a permanent community grouped under a chief man, the more favoured Saxon idea.

Evidence of the late development of many of these villages is contained in their place-names. Early village names tend to include the name of the original chief man or founder of the community; the many Saxon names terminating in -ing ('the people of . . .'), -ingham and -ington which are to be found everywhere in southern and eastern England are among the oldest in the country. Examples taken at random are Hastings, the 'people of Hæsta', who settled in Sussex at least as early as the eighth century (they are mentioned by the chronicler Simeon of Durham in 771); Rockingham (Northamptonshire), a name of the ninth century or probably earlier, the ham or village of Hroca's people; and Tredington (Warwickshire), the tun of Tyrdda's people, first mentioned in 757. Such foundations, and especially the -ings and -inghams, are among the earliest in England.

Having now reduced most of the English villages to three categories, I must appear to be inconsistent and say that it would be ridiculous to try to confine every village rigorously within these limits, to see each village as conforming to one or other of the three types and nothing more. A few may appear to conform absolutely to the pattern, but the majority have strayed outside it, while others are difficult to classify at all. Coastal villages, for example, are conditioned by their relationship to their harbours and their position in a valley or on a cliffside, and cannot easily be included in any generalisation. The form and size of most settlements, in fact, varied considerably from the norm. A nucleated character for some village may have been ruled out or modified by the progress of colonisation in its particular area. Contemporary descriptions of the Anglo-Saxon village, few though they are, only serve to emphasise this. Indeed, the innumerable variations in the plan of the village is one of the most fascinating characteristics of the English countryside.

The Viking Settlement

The Viking or Scandinavian conquest of eastern England, which took place from the ninth century onward, meant that a great many more villages were brought into being. The new invaders, who came mostly from Denmark, landed on the east coast between the Tyne and the Thames, and by 871 had overrun East Anglia and Mercia (the Midlands) and much of Northumbria. In 878, Alfred of Wessex, after

5 Cavendish, Suffolk

a successful counter-attack, signed a treaty which confined the Vikings to the region north-east of Watling Street. Yorkshire was then partitioned by them into Ridings ('thirdings') and that part of Mercia inside the Viking boundary, known as the Danelaw, came under the jurisdiction of the five newly-created boroughs of Nottingham, Derby, Leicester, Stamford and Lincoln. The beginning of the Viking settlement can be dated from about this time, but as the east Midlands were completely reconquered by the Anglo-Saxons under Edward the Elder (901-25), the settlements in this region must have been founded in the space of a little over 40 years. To the north of the Humber, the Viking kingdom flourished much longer (until 1066, in fact). In the tenth century, bands of Norwegians arrived in the north-west, chiefly around the Lake District, and they have left evidence of their settlements in the place-names of the region—the 'dales', 'thwaites' and so on. I shall come back to these in our regional survey, as the influence of the Norsemen, though important, was limited.

In some parts of eastern England, the Vikings outnumbered the native English, as we could by now reasonably call the Anglo-Saxons. Though the new settlers took over some of the villages vacated by the English who retreated westward, their arrival also resulted in a great intensification in districts as yet untouched by their predecessors. This in turn led to the foundation of new villages, as well as to many new hamlets and farmsteads away from the existing villages. Other settlements were the outcome of the accentuation in the drainage of the marsh and fen lands at this time.

With our present knowledge, we cannot decide how many villages were in fact established by the newcomers, for although Scandinavian names can easily be recognised (those ending in *by* are the most common), we do not know in how many instances the new settlers took over an existing Anglo-Saxon village (or even town) and gave it a new name. Derby, for example, one of the boroughs of the Danelaw, might be thought to have a Viking origin. Its name is Old Scandinavian and means 'town or village with a deer enclosure', or at least where deer were to be seen. But it was in fact previously known to the Saxons as 'Northworthy'. (In their place-names, incidentally, neither the Saxons nor the Vikings made any distinction between a town and a village.)

In some cases a village had a new name imposed on it by its neigh-

6 *West Hagbourne, Berkshire*
7 *Dorchester, Oxfordshire*

bours after it had been taken over by the Vikings. As an example, Wigston, in Leicestershire (quoted by Dr Hoskins), was called 'Viking's *tun*' after some Scandinavian leader. From this you might justifiably assume it to be a foundation of the Viking period, but an Anglo-Saxon cemetery was brought to light close to the village in the eighteenth century, and finds of the early (heathen) period from this proved that Wigston was already in existence, under some unknown name, long before the Vikings came.

There is no evidence that the Vikings changed the old English way of life to any degree or introduced any new type of village in the north and east, any more than they appear to have brought in any new methods of cultivation. As Sir Frank Stenton says: 'The field-names of Scandinavian origin, which are scattered in vast numbers over this country, illustrate the character of the settlement, but do not prove that it led to any material changes in agricultural practice.'

Much work needs to be done on excavating villages of presumed Viking origin, especially those that were deserted early in the Middle Ages, before we can say definitely what changes the settlers may have brought about. The inability to recognise any distinctively Viking contribution may indeed be the result of changes that have taken place in the village over the last thousand years and have consequently obscured if not obliterated the basic differences in plan. As we see them now, however, there is nothing in what appear to be Viking foundations of the ninth and tenth centuries that marks them out as being different in appearance from the Anglo-Saxon foundations.

Practically nothing now stands to give us any idea of what a village looked like in Saxon and Viking times. The only structures surviving from before the Norman Conquest are the remains of a relatively few parish churches. From at least the sixth century onward, churches were being built all over England, and several hundreds, if not a few thousands, were in existence before the coming of the Normans. In the limestone belt of Northamptonshire and other regions where good building stone could be obtained, some of these churches were large and handsome; examples are to be seen in Brixworth and the towers of Earls Barton and Barnack. More characteristic examples of Saxon stone building are the little church at Escomb and the chancels of Monkwearmouth and Jarrow, all in County Durham.

It is certain that over the greater part of the country, the Saxon church was little more than an unpretentious timber hut. The nave of Greenstead church, in Essex, the only surviving Saxon timber building in England, though restored, probably gives us a good impression of the average church of that time. This was undoubtedly dark and cheerless, and there is no reason to suppose that the houses in a Saxon village were any better—they were almost certainly not as good. Few of the smaller Saxon buildings would be constructed of durable material. Assuming on the one hand that greater care would be lavished on the church, and taking into account on the other the susceptibility of timber buildings to fire, life in the average Saxon dwelling must have been nasty and brutish, if not short.

Norman Influences on the Village

The coming of the Normans made very little difference to either the life or the structure of the English village. It is true that the Norman occupation had a profound effect on the English land system, but that influence was confined to law and property and did not extend to the pattern of agriculture. The invaders, after all, comprised a comparatively small upper class; the Conquest was essentially a military and political operation, not a migration of peoples. Though the new Norman overlords were responsible for the growth of some villages round their castles and, to a lesser extent, their ecclesiastical foundations, the overwhelming number of villages in England survived from an earlier date. Since the departure of the Romans, military considerations have never been of great importance in the English countryside, and life for the average English villager continued very much as before.

Domesday Book, compiled in 1086, is the earliest publication to give us a factual account of the state of the country (or most of it). By this time, the total population of England was reckoned at about a million and a quarter, and about nine people out of every ten still lived outside the towns or 'boroughs'. (Such towns as existed, in fact, were mostly small and scarcely to be distinguished from villages, except that they might be protected by a simple earthen fortification or rampart.)

We cannot tell how many 'countrymen' actually lived in villages and not in isolated hamlets or farmsteads, but it must have been a very large proportion. Domesday Book unfortunately does not reveal, either, what area of each county had been settled and how much still remained as 'waste' land. Though vast areas yet remained in their natural state, it is certain that the great majority of the villages we see today, as well as a number of others that have disappeared for one reason or another, were in existence by 1086. Apart from the evidence of *Domesday Book*, a study of their place-names is sufficient to prove this. In those districts of England that were still densely wooded at this time, some villages which now appear on the map were not founded until the twelfth or thirteenth century. Except for these and for the villages (comparatively few) newly created in the north and midlands during the Industrial Revolution, the general layout of the English villages looked very much as it does today.

But despite this widespread settlement, the country was still very sparsely settled by modern standards. Only six counties could muster more than 50,000 people each (the Domesday survey did not cover the four northernmost counties, of course, but these were among the most thinly inhabited). Norfolk, the most populous county in England at the time of Domesday, had only about 95,000 inhabitants (about one-quarter of its present population). Lincolnshire was next with some 90,000, while Suffolk and Devonshire had each about 70,000. Essex and Somerset each numbered between 50,000 and 60,000, and Kent, Sussex, Hampshire and Wiltshire had each between 40,000 and 50,000. Nottinghamshire, one of the last counties to be settled, had only about 20,000 inhabitants, while Yorkshire, which suffered grievously in its resistance to the Normans, had rather fewer than 30,000 inhabitants, despite its size.

Looked at another way, only Norfolk and Suffolk are recorded as having more than 12 *adults* to the square mile in the Domesday survey. In a great belt of country, stretching from Lincolnshire to Dorset and Somerset in one direction and to Kent and Essex in another, there were eight adults or over per square mile. At the other end of the scale, Derbyshire, Staffordshire, Shropshire and Cornwall had not more than four adults to the square mile, while Cheshire, Lancashire and Yorkshire had less than two. Though these figures do not tell us how many people were living in villages or give any indication what the 'average' size of a village was, they do show which regions were the main centres of prosperity at the beginning of the Norman era.

When we come to consider the populations of the actual villages, the records are very incomplete and they have to be treated with great diffidence, due allowance being made for human limitations as well as for possible local variations in the methods of obtaining the information. The recorded populations for 12 villages in Cambridgeshire, for instance, vary from 12 to 82, but whether this includes every human being in each case, women and children as well as the 'productive' men, it is impossible to say (the Domesday survey was of course primarily concerned with the state of agriculture). Some of the villages in eastern England seem to have been quite large; several in Lincolnshire had more than 30 sokemen's or freemen's houses (no account was taken here of the unfree villeins).

Perhaps the most noticeable effect of the Norman Conquest on the existing English villages is the addition to many of their names of a distinguishing attribute, usually derived from the name of the Norman overlord and indicating, if nothing else, that the English villager had now exchanged his Saxon or Viking master for a Norman one. Over 700 villages with common English names have a Norman addition; by far the greater number are in the south-western counties and most of these are in Somerset, which can claim no fewer than 78. As Professor Tait observed in one of the English Place-Name Society's volumes, 'Bagpuize, Bowells, Bubb, Coggles, Crubb, Goose, Gubbals, Puddock, Pudding and Wallop rub shoulders with Champflower, Courtenay, Curson, D'Evercy, Grandison, Lancelyn, Longueville, Monchensie, Montague, Morieux, St Quentin and Seymour.' At first these additions must have been nearly all in French, but as the Normans settled down in their new land and began to take their territorial designations from their manors, and as the landed classes increasingly drew their numbers from the native English, so many more English names began to find their way in.

Early Medieval Developments

The work of clearing the impenetrable woodland and converting it into arable land, begun by the Anglo-Saxons and continued by the Anglicised Vikings, went on apace after the Norman Conquest. New farms and hamlets, with their fields, continued to be made by small bands of settlers out of the waste. In the north and west of England especially, there were more isolated hamlets and farmsteads, in remote clearings, than there were villages. From Yorkshire to Devonshire, dozens of place-names testify to the clearance of the woodlands in the twelfth and thirteenth centuries: nearly all the numerous Woodhouses, Woodhalls, Woodcotes and Woodmancotes and many of the Newlands and New-halls will be found to date from this time.

Though many of the clearings never supported more than a single farmstead or at most a hamlet of a few cottages, some of these became the centres of parishes with their own churches serving a scattered loosely-bound community of farmsteads and cottages. But sometimes whole new villages were created in the clearings. Such villages are particularly common in the north Midlands, where the thick woods of the heavy clay country now began to be cleared. Mansfield, in Notting-hamshire, for instance, is mentioned in *Domesday Book*, but the outpost of Mansfield Woodhouse is first heard of in 1230. Woodhouse Eaves in Charnwood Forest is mentioned for the first time between 1209 and 1235.

One characteristic of the Norman infiltration that increased in effect during the early Middle Ages was the infusing of a livelier spirit into the whole ecclesiastical life of the country. Several thousand churches were built (or rebuilt) in the two centuries following the Conquest, the majority of them during the hundred years after 1150. About this time the division of England into parishes was completed, and the church became more than before a visible centre and symbol of the village community.

Most of these early parish churches, especially in the more remote districts, were simple unpretentious buildings, usually of rubble masonry, material from the local stonepit, erected by the labour of the villagers themselves. But in the larger and more prosperous villages, churches became progressively bigger and were invariably built of stone blocks. Though bricks were made in eastern England from at least the thirteenth century onward, they were not employed to any great extent until two centuries later. Even then, they were reserved for the larger houses and town churches; they were still too expensive for the fabric of village churches.

Sometimes the building of the church was paid for by the lord of the manor or by an interested ecclesiastical foundation (perhaps itself the landowner) and the result most likely was a larger and more elaborate structure. But in some parts of England, by the fourteenth century at least, the villagers themselves were rather less ground down by poverty and they showed their appreciation in a series of splendid parish churches. This is particularly notable along or near the broad limestone belt running from Lincoln to Somerset, where the noble oolitic building stone displays itself in a constellation of magnificent towers and spires.

By the end of the thirteenth century, the process of settlement was very largely completed and the map of England could show the same names, though in a variety of spellings, as it does today. Then, as now, the village settlement lay thickest in the east and south; in the northern part of Norfolk, where the Fens still cut off further westward advance, the villages were placed closer together than anywhere else in the country. In the Fenland, on the other hand, and in the uncultivated moorland districts of the north and west, they were still sparsely distributed. In the chalk country of the south, villages stretched like beads on a cord at the foot of the escarpments of the Chiltern Hills, the Berkshire Downs, and the North and South Downs, as well as along the river valleys, though there were few on the upland plateaux. But over most of England, the medieval traveller would have noticed that villages followed each other at fairly regular intervals.

The Black Death and the Depopulation of the Villages

Though England still possessed many wild and uncultivated districts, the great labour of deforestation and colonisation that had gone on unchecked since the Conquest must have made it look a very settled country by the middle of the fourteenth century. But in 1348 the first of a series of events occurred which was to change the landscape and have a profound effect on English village life. This was the beginning of those attacks of bubonic plague known as the Black Death.

The population of England had grown to something like four millions, about three times what it had been when *Domesday Book* was compiled. In the ten generations since the Norman invasion, hundreds of thousands of acres of cleared land had been brought under cultivation. In less than two years, the successive outbreaks of the plague reduced the population by more than one-third and perhaps by as much as one-half. This resulted in a wholesale retreat from the farmsteads, hamlets and even villages along the margins of cultivation, where the settlements were still comparatively poor and thin. Every part of England was affected by the plague: families died off, land lay untilled, hamlets and cottages were deserted. Some villages were completely devastated and never reoccupied; others were abandoned and the survivors moved to new sites some distance off. Reduced in morale as well as in numbers, they chose to settle in the smaller hamlets, leaving the old villages to decay.

Though this book is concerned with living villages, not dead ones, it is worth while devoting a few paragraphs to the fascinating subject of deserted villages, especially as these throw an unusual light on other changes that were imminent at this time. M. W. Beresford, in *The Lost Villages of England*, says that the sites of more than 1,300 deserted villages have been located. Most of these are in the 'Lowland Zone' of the midlands and eastern England. In the three counties of Warwickshire, Leicestershire and Northamptonshire alone about 250 village sites have been found. In Lincolnshire there are nearly 150, in Norfolk 130 and in the East Riding of Yorkshire about 100. The number of known sites is less in the hilly regions of the north and west, not simply owing to fewer villages having been established in these regions, but also because the settlements were generally smaller and consequently are more difficult to locate.

The Black Death was not the first cause (though it might be the worst) of the wholesale depopulation of these villages. The enclosing of the royal forests—such as the New Forest—begun soon after the Norman Conquest, had meant the extermination of the villages and hamlets within their confines. Then from the twelfth century onward, the establishment of monastic houses and granges, particularly those of the Cistercian order, resulted in other early desertions. The Cistercians usually settled in unclaimed country and brought it under cultivation, but sometimes they demolished a village or hamlet to secure a favourable tract of country for themselves. The village of Upper Smite in Warwickshire, for instance, was pulled down in about 1150 to give space for the building of Combe Abbey.

Over and above these deliberate exterminations, however, there were other villages, settled in difficult and unremunerative country, that were always on the edge of failure and collapse, and the Black Death dealt the final blow to many of these. All over the country there were villages which were unable to keep going and which have now com-

8 *Castle Acre, Norfolk*

pletely disappeared except perhaps for a solitary and even fragmentary church and the grassy banks and hollows that mark the positions of their houses and streets. Around the edges of the barren region of Breckland, in East Anglia, no fewer than 28 abandoned villages have been discovered. Most of these probably never flourished at any time, but the plague put paid to the unrewarding efforts to keep them going. Even so, the unfortunate villagers struggled on: the desertions extended in some cases over three or four generations and the last of these villages were not abandoned until the fifteenth century.

The final stages in the desertion of some villages were hastened by the landowners themselves, whether these were laymen or monasteries. The reduced population was inadequate to maintain the arable farmlands on which the village and its landlord depended. This reduction, as it happened, coincided with a big increase in the demand for land for pasturing cattle and sheep, which required only a comparatively small proportion of the labour needed for arable farming. What could be easier than to evict the dwindling survivors of the village, demolish their dwellings—a simple operation, as they were mostly of mud walls, with thatched roofs and rubble foundations—and convert the village and its fields into a large enclosure for pastoral farming?

The Black Death reduced the population of England by a million and a half or more and had a crippling effect on the country's economy. For many villages the century following the outbreaks of the plague was a period of retreat and decay. But thousands of villages survived or recovered from the scourge and began to look forward to a new prosperity. The economic decline had struck hardest at the midlands, where the development in the previous century had been greatest, but the north and west, where the settlements were smaller and farther apart, and where the villager, attuned to a harder life, had become perhaps more resilient, were less affected by the plague. In such parts of England land continued to be rescued from the wilds and brought under cultivation. The name of Horsley Woodhouse, in Derbyshire, first mentioned in 1431, is one of those indicating that settlement was still going on.

The Wool Trade and the Resurgence of the Village

The great movement which caused a revolution in English agriculture and had the most profound influence on village life made its effect felt

9 *Groton, Suffolk*
10 *Thaxted, Essex*

mainly in the south and east. I have already mentioned that pastoral farming was gaining ground at the expense of arable. Apart from this, the open-field system of agriculture with its three-crop rotation cycle, carried on almost unchanged since the coming of the Saxons, was proving more and more wasteful, and there was a growing pressure in favour of enclosure. But despite the gradual lapse of the common-land system, coupled with the legal practice which since the Norman Conquest had given waste lands into the possession of the overlords, it needed the stimulus of some new development in agriculture to spur the demand for enclosure to any marked extent.

This development was the direct result of the wool trade, which had originated in eastern England as early as the twelfth century and had now become of national importance. At first, the raw material had been exported to Flanders for manufacture into cloth there, but after the accession of Edward III in 1327 a new policy was adopted. A native cloth-making industry was established, with the aid of immigrant Flemish weavers, and eventually this not only absorbed all the wool grown in this country but home-produced cloth became by far the most important export.

By the end of the Middle Ages, though the population had increased again to nearly three millions, sheep outnumbered human beings by about three to one. The growth of the wool trade and the consequent demand for more pasture and in turn for root-crops for sheep had inspired a further demand for enclosure. (This was later enhanced by the confiscation of the monastic lands and their transfer to wealthy new landowners.) By the sixteenth century, the south and east of England, and especially the great wool-growing districts, were among the richest agricultural regions in Europe.

The tremendous development in sheep farming led to great sheep walks being created, particularly in the midland and eastern counties, the west country and west Yorkshire. Flocks increased rapidly until it was estimated that there were as many as 150,000 sheep in East Anglia alone. Sheep farming, especially on a large scale, involved considerably less expenditure than arable farming and it showed a far greater return. It is reckoned that by about 1550 half a million acres had been turned over from arable to pastoral farming, and some 50,000 farm workers had lost their livelihood. But although the average villager suffered, at least in the wool-growing districts, trade prospered as a whole and a new class of yeoman farmer who had turned wool production into a capitalist enterprise began to appear.

This is not a history of agriculture, so I will say no more about the enormous effect of the wool trade. But the revolution showed itself in the English village in two ways: in the great rebuilding of the medieval parish church, and in the consequent rebuilding of the village itself during the general period of prosperity that followed in the sixteenth century.

Medieval Village Building

Apart from its church, and occasionally its manor house (usually much restored), practically nothing of the medieval village now remains to be seen. This, however, is certainly no great loss. The rural population in the Middle Ages must have been housed in conditions that bear a closer resemblance to the mud villages of central Africa than to those villages that charm us today. The houses were generally of mud, wattle and thatch, and few of them would be as picturesque as the cottages of a later period which have survived in these materials. Very few houses were constructed of stone, even in country where stone was readily obtainable. The houses may have had a timber framework, where timber was easily procurable, but the rooms had no ceilings (they were open to the rafters), there was only one fireplace, and the windows were not glazed but were mere holes in the walls, possibly latticed. Sometimes the only aperture was the door, apart perhaps from a hole in the roof to let the smoke out. The typical medieval dwelling was in truth a squalid and flimsy hovel, dark, cramped and probably damp.

Even in London the ordinary houses were so insubstantial that in the thirteenth century the Aldermen of the City were provided with crooks so that they could pull them down when they caught fire. Where the house had a timber framework, this was usually pre-fabricated in sections, but rarely were the houses built on any solid foundation. A thirteenth-century manuscript qualifies a wooden house 'whether it be attached to the ground or not', and another document declares that 'anyone who shall receive certain heretics shall have his house carried outside the town and burnt'. If the town house was like this, how much more primitive was the average country dwelling?

The open-field system, too, could hardly be considered an aesthetic asset to the village. Except for the village gardens and stockyards, such as they were, nothing was enclosed. The common arable land, meadow-land and waste land surrounding the village were all open. Imagine an England devoid of those neat hedges with their occasional rows of trees which are today a characteristic feature of the rural scene, with all the fields much larger and divided only by low banks of earth, a mass of tangled scrubland on the outskirts and a squalid village in the centre, and you have the essentials of the medieval country scene.

The chief contribution of the Middle Ages to the village as we see it today is its church. In the century or more before 1500, hundreds of parish churches were rebuilt or enlarged in England. By the end of the Middle Ages there were few villages without a stone-built church and the majority of these or the greater parts of them have happily survived to the present day.

Very few churches were rebuilt during this period in the midlands, where, as I have said, the agricultural depression resulting from the Black Death was felt most acutely. But in the thriving wool areas in particular, new and splendid churches were created; some of the very finest churches in the country are the outcome of the great prosperity in local industry. Wealthy wool merchants and clothiers frequently paid for the entire rebuilding of their parish churches. To the sheep which grazed above the East Anglian chalk and the Cotswold lime-stone we owe the noble churches of these regions.

Perpendicular Gothic, expressive of the affluence of the age, became the predominant style. Magnificent towers raised themselves everywhere above the village, but especially in Somerset, Suffolk and the East Riding. In the limestone country of Northamptonshire and Rutland, too, the Gothic parish church attained a perfect harmony of all its parts and seems to grow naturally from the ground on which it stands.

Not all parishes, of course, had the necessary resources to rebuild or even enlarge their churches. Those of the south-east, for instance, from Essex to Hampshire, are mostly of the humbler sort, though here, just as much, they seem to grow from their native roots. In Essex, brickwork had come into use before the close of the Middle Ages; it is to be seen in many church towers and porches and even occasionally in the walls. The smaller and simpler these village structures, the more they were likely to be dependent on local materials and influenced by local traditions. The men who built these village churches were local craftsmen, not architects with offices in London, and until the age of the railway, local material was the cheapest. Only the builders of the cathedrals and town churches, or the larger village churches paid for by the newly rich, could afford to have their materials transported from any distance.

By the end of the Middle Ages, with the general increase in wealth that was beginning to affect even the village labourer, houses were becoming more substantial. A method of construction widely used, especially in well-wooded districts, was the 'cruck'. This consisted basically of two large curved pieces of timber, one end of each of which rested on the ground or a stone base, while the other ends supported each other at the top. Two pairs of crucks were then joined together by a horizontal ridge timber, rather resembling a tent, and round these the whole house was fashioned. The rafters were originally thatched over to make a continuous roof, from the ridge pole to the ground, but a later development was to rest the rafters on horizontal lengths of timber, called wall plates, at a height above the ground, these being supported by cross-beams or tie-beams bracing each pair of crucks. By this means a wall could be arranged between the roof and the ground and hence more room given to the interior of the house. The 'cruck' form of construction continued into Tudor times and examples are still to be seen here and there, especially in the midlands.

Tudor Expansion and Rebuilding

With the new wealth inspired by the wool trade, a great change came over the English landscape. The country was at long last recovering from the decline brought about by the Black Death and aggravated by the Wars of the Roses. The population began to rise rapidly, for the first time for nearly two hundred years; industries were flourishing and trade was expanding in new directions. The production of food became a problem for an increasingly thriving and vigorous nation. As the demand for corn and other foodstuffs improved, mixed farming steadily regained its balance, and there was a growing demand, too, for other country products, such as leather. Farmers as well as wool merchants in fact had 'never had it so good', and this general prosperity percolated through to the average villager. During the Elizabethan age, in particular, the village thrived as it had never done before. Except in the more northerly counties, which enjoyed their period of prosperity later, a great wave of rebuilding swept over the country between about 1570 and 1640.

The change was ushered in with a great demand for country houses on the part of the newly rich of Henry VIII's reign. The impetus created by this soon began to make itself felt among the other classes and by the 1560's the more affluent freeholder or yeoman farmer was building himself a larger and finer house. Sometimes the ancestral home was enlarged and reconstructed; more often than not, it was pulled down to make way for a more substantial and more comfortable house, built in freestone where this was readily available, though brick was now coming into favour for the larger houses.

Before the end of the sixteenth century, the fashion for rebuilding had reached the lesser farmers, and no doubt the more prosperous of the villagers were also prompted to try their hands at the exciting new venture. It must not be thought, however, that the poorer villagers who made up the bulk of the rural population could attempt to rebuild on any elaborate scale. Outside the great wool-producing areas, certainly, cottages were still built by the landlords in a cheap and rather shoddy manner. Few small cottages, if any, seem to have survived intact from the sixteenth century or earlier. The 'olde worlde Tudor cottage' advertised by the estate-agent, if indeed it dates from as early as this, is more likely to have been a yeoman farmer's house.

The great urge towards country building increased in momentum until the opening of the Civil War in 1642. The villages of the midlands and eastern counties in particular contain innumerable yeomen's houses built during the last years of Elizabeth I and the reigns of the first two Stewarts, and the famous 'black-and-white' timber-framed manor houses of the Western marches almost all belong to this period. On or near the rich limestone belt, whole villages were rebuilt in stone about the same time, but evidence of the Great Rebuilding (as Dr Hoskins has called it) can be seen all over the more prosperous parts of England.

This rich flowering of rural building, in what may truly be called the vernacular style, was the outcome not only of the new acquisition of wealth, but of the greater desire for comfort and privacy. The countryman had taken discomfort as a matter of course in the Middle Ages, but before the advent of the Tudors the fortified castle was already giving way to the domestic manor house, and this change had a strong influence on the new middle classes in England. No longer did all the household, from the lord to the lowest servant, congregate in the great hall, as in feudal times. In numerous houses surviving from medieval times, the hall and other barn-like rooms open to the rafters were divided by having another floor inserted and partitions put up to make smaller, more compact apartments. A method of producing cheap glass had been discovered, too, and this brought it within reach of the less wealthy classes. As a result, more windows could be provided and most were glazed for the first time.

This desire for greater comfort expressed itself among the yeomen farmers, who marked their new affluence in the beautiful houses they built themselves. Of all the secular buildings in the English landscape, none are more photogenic than those of the 70 years up to the outbreak of the Civil War. In these three generations the regional styles came to display a rich variety, everywhere employing the local materials, but using them in such a way that the rural culture has never reached such a level of beauty and dignity. It is in this village building, and, to a lesser extent, in the second great rebuilding that began in the late seventeenth century, that we find the most satisfying qualities of vernacular architecture.

By the end of the sixteenth century, cruck construction was being replaced in the timber-framed house by the 'box-frame' or 'post and truss' method. On a stone, brick or hard clay foundation was laid a horizontal timber beam, with sockets at intervals for upright posts, which were socketed at the top into another horizontal beam called a head-piece. The spaces were then filled in with 'wattle and daub', consisting of hazel branches, osiers or brushwood woven together to form a matrix and plastered over with clay. The distance between the upright posts was necessarily small at first, but as timber became scarcer, the spaces grew larger and an infilling of bricks (called 'nogging') was often adopted. In some later buildings, the whole of the lower storey is of brick.

The upper storeys of the building, similarly constructed, were supported on horizontal timbers called joists which sometimes projected over the lower storey (a feature known as 'jettying'). Several explanations have been put forward for this curious overhang, which is found in most parts of England, but especially in the south and east. The most plausible reason is that it was designed to give a clear drip and thus keep the ground floor dry. This would be of particular necessity when the walls were covered with plaster.

The Second Great Rebuilding

At the beginning of the seventeenth century, England was still a quiet agricultural country—the Industrial Revolution had not yet begun to make its mark on the landscape. Foreigners who visited this country saw it as a land of prosperity and plenty. One Venetian ambassador, writing in 1607, described Britain as 'comfortable, pleasant, and rich beyond all other islands in the world', and another wrote in 1622 that it was 'as fruitful in commerce as by the gifts of nature'. It is probable that these gentlemen did not take themselves out into the countryside much, but if they had they would have found it little changed in fundamentals since 1086.

Despite all the building that had been going on, the village looked in its essentials very much as it did during the Middle Ages. The yeoman lived in his farmhouse built of the local materials, which seems to us today a cottage; the labourer still occupied his small cabin (it was hardly anything more), rebuilt perhaps, but still rudimentary. In most places, farming had advanced but had not changed its methods since the later Middle Ages; open fields and commonland still enclosed the average village. The rural scene in fact still had to undergo a revolution.

But before this happened, a second great wave of rebuilding had swept forward in England. It started in the second half of the seventeenth century and continued well through the eighteenth. After the interlude of the Civil War and its aftermath, England was again prosperous, and this prosperity coincided with the growing use of brick for building. Some of the larger mansions had been built entirely in this material since the fifteenth century, but bricks were expensive to produce and consequently they were limited mostly to those districts where stone was difficult to obtain. But in the late seventeenth century, brick construction began to replace timber over a wide area, and particularly in the clay country. Not only were the supplies of good timber running low, but the rebuilding of London after the Great Fire, among other things, stimulated the demand for bricks, which could now be made much cheaper than before, using our many excellent clays. It was discovered, too, that brick buildings had other advantages: they were fireproof and they excluded vermin. Bricks were not only easy to handle, but it was found they could be used for ornamentation, as we can see from many of the handsome buildings of this period that have survived.

The art of brick-making, which seems to have been lost with the departure of the Romans, was reintroduced from the Netherlands, and it reached the eastern counties first, no doubt because of the trading connections with this part of England. The influence of the Netherlands showed itself in the change over from English bond (alternate courses of headers and stretchers) to Flemish bond (stretchers and headers arranged alternately in each row). Though English bond is in fact stronger, Flemish bond has a neater appearance.

Flemish influence was also the inspiration of some of the details to be seen in the buildings of this time: the round curves of the gable ends in East Anglia, for instance, and the crow-stepped work seen in the church porches, and occasionally the houses, in Essex. But everywhere houses were being built or rebuilt in brick. To this period, too, we owe many of our early brick-built schools, chapels and almshouses. At the same time, stone was not being neglected in those regions where it was still easy to quarry. The graziers of the midlands, for example, taking advantage of their enhanced prosperity, were engaged on ambitious schemes of rebuilding that are reflected in the villages; Rockingham, in Northamptonshire, mostly rebuilt between 1660 and 1720, is one example of how attractive a village of this period can be.

Until the Industrial Revolution, the making of cloth was largely a village industry, carried on by the weavers and their families in their own homes and on their own looms. In the fifteenth and sixteenth centuries cloth-making had been centred particularly in East Anglia, Kent, the Cotswolds and Somerset, though its effect was widespread in the south. But in the seventeenth century it started to move up-country to the north midlands and the north, and whole villages here began to be turned over to industry. The weavers' houses are mostly to be distinguished by the long, uninterrupted window on the upper floor giving light to the room in which the weaving frame stood. The stone cottages of this kind which are a speciality of the West Riding I have dealt with in the appropriate place.

Allied industries, too, were carried on in the northern half of England, continuing to occupy village craftsmen until well into the nineteenth century. Bedworth (now a colliery town) and Bulkington, in north Warwickshire, are two of the places where the three-storey houses, their lofty upper rooms lit by large windows, are a reminder of the silk-weaving industry that flourished in this neighbourhood in the eighteenth and early nineteenth centuries. A peculiarity of Leicestershire and Nottinghamshire are the brick stockingers' houses of the late eighteenth and early nineteenth centuries, of two storeys, and again with the long upper window. Needless to say, such early industrial villages bear only the remotest resemblance to the hideous industrial conglomerations of the later nineteenth century.

The Agricultural Revolution

I said that the English scene still had to undergo a revolution to transform it from the open landscape into the patchwork of small fields we are familiar with today. This great change was brought about by the enclosure acts of about 1750 onward. In some regions the transformation had already taken place: in Kent and Essex, Devon and Cornwall, and to some extent in Somerset and Suffolk, many of the fields had been enclosed in the Middle Ages for fruit-farming or some other local activity, where they had not been reclaimed direct from moorland or forest. But over much of England the rural scene was still medieval in character.

In the 60 years of George III's reign, enclosure by act of parliament revitalised the rural economy. Between 1760 and 1815 a total of nearly 2,000 enclosure acts was passed, affecting as many as 3,000 parishes, it is said, and about $5\frac{1}{2}$-million acres of land. The open fields were first divided with the idea of improving the productivity of the land; then the commons and waste land were taken in to bring new land under cultivation. The pattern of field and hedgerow or drystone wall established itself as we know it today. Though the enclosures concerned almost the whole of England, they were most pronounced in the prosperous districts of the midlands and the eastern counties.

With the enclosure of the open fields, land was mostly redistributed in detached compact blocks, replacing the strips scattered about all over the parish. In consequence, many farms had to be created away from the centre of the village, where they had persisted since Saxon times, and it may reasonably be asked why the old village based on the open-field economy did not disintegrate. One answer is that enclosure had been a costly business, and although the wealthier grazier could build himself a new farmhouse, the smaller man could not afford to, but continued to live in the village and work the farm from a distance. Often enough, he carried out few repairs to his house and when it became untenable he built himself a new farmhouse among his own fields. This explains why one sees so many nineteenth-century farmhouses and also why so many village houses had to be rebuilt. There was nothing wrong with the sixteenth- and seventeenth-century houses and more would have survived if they had been kept in good repair.

There was another reason why the village did not fall apart after the enclosures. With the growth of the yeoman farmer class and the capitalisation of agriculture, the land everywhere was divided among fewer owners than it had been in the Middle Ages. As a result, there were naturally fewer farmers who might wish to build out in the fields. But in any case, having a larger tract of land and more labourers to work it, the farmer could afford to continue to operate from the village. At the same time, the population was rising over the whole country, and there was a greater demand for houses. The Industrial Revolution, too, was beginning to show its hand, and in some places the farmhouses which the yeomen had quitted could very well be adapted to suit the workers in the growing village industries.

Despite these and other changes that had taken place in the countryside in more than 700 years, the distribution of English villages remained very similar to what it had been in 1086. The traveller at the end of the eighteenth century, once he had left behind the outskirts of the towns (and these, except for London, were still comparatively small), passed through a landscape dotted with villages, hamlets and farmsteads, hardly more thickly spread than in Norman times. Here and there he saw nucleated villages, their dwellings forming compact groups, usually round the parish church; elsewhere he found dispersed hamlets, farmsteads and (to a growing extent) country mansions. These 'gentlemen's seats', as the early topographers called them, were mostly built well away from the villages, but with the growing affluence of the aristocracy in the eighteenth century they became larger and grander, and their parks became larger, too, and had to be 'landscaped'. Not only did the village fields disappear behind the park walls, but in some cases the village itself was destroyed or transplanted when it offended the wealthy landowner or stood in the way of his schemes. Examples of re-sited villages are Milton Abbas in Dorset and Edensor in Derbyshire, moved to suit the pleasure of the Earl of Dorchester and the Duke of Devonshire respectively.

The Effects of the Industrial Revolution

But, as I have already hinted, another change was taking place in the English countryside. Defoe, in his *Tour through England and Wales*, written in 1724–6, described vividly not only those regions that had always been prosperous, such as East Anglia, but also the lesser-known parts such as the Pennine valleys, where industry was already supporting a larger population. The economy of a growing number of villages began to depend, not so much on agriculture, as on the development of some branch of the weaving industry. This was the start of a movement that was to grow almost unnoticed (except by such acute observers as Defoe) until it became the full tide of the Industrial Revolution.

Industries dependent on the country for their basic materials were carried on in villages at first, as I suggested in talking about the weavers' houses-cum-workshops. Only as the industries developed were they transferred to towns, though of course some of the villages grew into towns themselves, while others—an even worse fate—were absorbed in the near-by towns as these grew. The Industrial Revolution, by introducing powered machinery and hence necessitating the concentration of workers in factories, effectively destroyed the village industries. Worse than that, they not only made an end of the spinning and other part-time employment of the agricultural families, they also put out of work the full-time village craftsman. In the course of some 170 years after the accession of George III, industry was transferred almost completely from the village to the town. The result was a large-scale emigration of the villager, with his skill and craftsmanship, to the town, and the reduction of the village to a purely agricultural community, with an inevitable narrowing of the villager's outlook and independence.

Until the Industrial Revolution, building construction in England had always followed an evolutionary path, and this was particularly true of village building. Every new style was related to the past; every new method was a development of an existing one. In the eighteenth century, design in our English villages reached its maturity. Cottages had improved out of all recognition both in their construction and their finish; they were not only better built, they were better proportioned. The larger farm and manor houses of this period display a high degree of elegance and urbanity. Village building of all kinds had come a long way since the Middle Ages, when the discomfort of cramped quarters, smoke and draughts was taken as the natural order of things.

The great development of towns during the eighteenth century led to a proportionate increase in the use of brick, and the popularisation in the towns of the classical forms, for which brick was eminently suited, made its influence felt in much of the new village building. Traditional brick building had always been attractive, and indeed it still is in the clay country in which brick is the natural product. But the opening up of the countryside by the railways resulted in an almost universal demand for cheap bricks, to the great detriment of rural building. Once it became cheaper and easier to transport bricks to, say, the Cotswolds than to quarry the local limestone, village building began to lose its character. All through the Victorian era, in fact, the quality and individuality of building deteriorated; the increase in mass-produced materials led to the growth of mass-produced houses, and a consequent further decline in the demand for the village craftsman, with his ability and knowledge, the fruit of generations of experience.

Our only satisfaction in all this is that so great a part of our villages survives from before the Industrial Revolution. If in its basic plan the village is still rooted in Anglo-Saxon England and in its church building it is a healthy survival of the Middle Ages, in its domestic buildings the English village still remains essentially the product of the period which extends from the Tudor to the Georgian era—say from about 1570 to 1770. This was the period of domestic architecture which beautified the village, and after it village architecture failed to improve the face of nature.

English Villages
A Regional Survey

HAVING CONSIDERED, briefly and, I am afraid, superficially, the 'past' of the English village—the factors and influences that have caused it to assume the shape and style we are familiar with—I now go on to look at the 'present', the varied pattern and structure of our villages as they are today.

For this survey, I have divided the country into fourteen regions. These, as I said in the Preamble, are determined largely by their geological structure, but in some regions I have overlooked the geological considerations and favoured a geographical division. This is partly because the geological pattern here is too complex to be broken up, but also because in some regions—Devon and Cornwall, East Yorkshire and the North-West are examples—the geographical pattern is the more important. In East Yorkshire, for instance, the villages around the chalk and limestone bear a much closer relation to each other than they do to those of the chalk of Wiltshire or the limestone of the Cotswolds. The Yorkshire villages are not pale reflections of the villages farther south, as some writers have implied; they are fundamentally different.

The map at the beginning of the book shows the divisions I have made, in relation to relevant towns.

1 The Weald and Greensand Country

The Weald of Kent, Surrey and Sussex, taking its name from the Anglo-Saxon 'wald', meaning woodland, is geologically a region of mixed sandstones and clays, surrounded by a rim of greensand except

where it is bordered by the English Channel or the alluvial flats of
Romney Marsh and the Pevensey Levels, between Eastbourne and
Folkestone. The greensand rim is enclosed in turn by the chalk of the
North and South Downs, the most familiar feature of south-east
England, described in Section 2.

The sands and clays of the Weald were at one time completely
covered by the great forest of Andredesweald, and this long supported
a flourishing iron-smelting industry. Based on the ironstone found in
the deposits, the industry was at its most prosperous during the
Middle Ages, though it persisted until the nineteenth century. The
forest was also the principal source of timber for our famous wooden
ships. In consequence, it was gradually cleared (though the Weald is
still comparatively well wooded) and the land was mostly converted to
agriculture. Today the orchards and hop-gardens of the Weald are
renowned.

The prosperity experienced as a result of the employment of these
resources, combined with the proximity of the Weald to London and
the Channel ports, and aided to some extent by the clothing industry
that began to thrive after Edward III invited refugee Flemings to settle
here, has always made the south-east of England a comfortable region,
and this sense of well-being is reflected in the careful building and neat
villages which are to be enjoyed everywhere in the Weald.

Before considering the villages, however, I must say a word or two
about the geological composition that has moulded them and the way
it has evolved. The south-east of England is split off from the rest of
the country geologically and its physical make-up is relatively easy to
understand. This is because the successive formations were deposited
directly one on top of another in layers, and were then forced up
along a line running east and west more or less through their centre, so
that the various strata came to be shaped like a series of arches,
resting on each other. The higher parts of the formations then started
to get worn away by the action of streams and weather, exposing the
older rocks underneath. The softer deposits were naturally worn
down to a much greater extent than the harder, with the result that the
harder formations, the chalk and the sandstones, now stand out as long
outcrops with well-defined crests or ridges running right across country
from east to west. Thus, as you travel from north to south over this
part of England—say from London to Brighton—you cross successively

the London clay (which comes into the third section of this survey), the chalk of the North Downs, the greensand hills, the Wealden clay (sometimes called the Vale of Kent, though it extends also into Surrey), the Wealden sands, another tract of the clay (the Vale of Sussex), a narrower belt of greensand, and finally the chalk of the South Downs before reaching the sea.

The centre of this group is occupied by the oldest formation, the Wealden Sands, or Hastings Sands as they are often named because they break down to the sea at that ancient town. Revealed by the denudation of all the strata that overlaid it, this hard, light-brown sandstone outcrop consists mainly of two long broken ranges of uplands, sometimes called the Forest Ridges, resolving themselves as a multiplicity of narrow ridges, separated by deep valleys watered by streams that have washed away the softer intermingling clays. This was the chief region of the ironworking industry.

Enclosing the Forest Ridges is a wide, gently-undulating basin of the Wealden Clay, a thick shaly formation, rather bluish or brownish in colour. This is surrounded in turn by the Lower Greensand, a rich brownish-yellow sandstone containing grains of glauconite, the hard greenish mineral which gives the outcrop its name and much of its character. In the south of our region, the greensand is of comparatively little importance, but in the north it shows itself as a striking range of hills, of which the best known are those between Leith Hill and Hindhead. This range, broken in places and varying considerably in height, stretches right across Kent and Surrey, within the rim of the North Downs and separated from the chalk by a series of narrow valleys.

Oddly enough, these hills have never acquired a well-known name. They have been called the Red Hills (but the colour of their soil is not red) and also the Ragstone Range, an ugly name. Some writers have misleadingly included them with the chalk North Downs, which are quite distinct, while others, equally confusingly, lump them with the Weald as though they were of the same structure. Elsewhere, I have referred to them as the Greensand Hills, and this is the name I shall continue to use.

The stone obtained from the Greensand Hills, frequently called Kentish Rag (the principal quarries are in Kent, around Maidstone), has been used a great deal for road-making, but has often been depre-

11 *Witley, Surrey*

cated as a building stone. It is not an easy stone to work, and some authorities have declared that it is too hard and brittle to be able to cut suitable blocks of freestone from it; the only use of this stone, they say, is for foundations and rubble walls. But the greensand quarries have provided stone not only for local building but also for Windsor Castle, Knole and other great houses, and Kentish rag has gone into many Kentish churches. Tall church towers of ragstone make prominent landmarks all over this part of the Weald, while in the western part there are many examples of villages whose houses are built of this sandstone.

At the foot of the chalk downs extends a thin belt of the Upper Greensand, a light brown sandstone known locally as firestone and quarried as building stone near Merstham, Godstone and other places in Surrey. Below this greensand is a grey-blue clay called Gault, from which light-coloured bricks are made. The rich Wealden clays, too, have provided ample material for bricks and tiles, and until the clearance of the great forest, there was timber in plenty. With the wealth of building material at their disposal, it is not surprising that there is a great variety of construction to be seen in the villages of the Weald and Greensand country. The high standard of living always enjoyed in this part of England, too, meant that the variety in materials could be combined with a high standard of craftsmanship, and the villages as a whole produce as satisfying an architectural effect as those of any part of England (incidentally making it more difficult for me to select from the many examples for the list that follows).

The characteristic cottages in the clay regions of the Weald are of the timber-framed, or half-timbered, type—a framework of massive oak timbers (elm or willow in the cheaper houses) with an infilling of lath and plaster or, more frequently, of bricks laid obliquely in alternate rows, called 'nogging' (flint is used occasionally where it can be readily obtained from the neighbouring chalk). The typical timber-framed building in the Weald makes use of closely-spaced uprights, as is usual in East Anglia, not the slanting timbers that are much more common in midland and western England, where timber construction is also conspicuous.

An ingenious and picturesque method of covering the outer walls in the Weald and Greensand country is by vertical tile-hanging (sometimes called 'weather-tiling'), a craft first introduced towards the end

12 *Near Smarden, Kent*
13 *Dunsford, Devonshire*

of the seventeenth century. The tiles, though similar to those used on the roof, show a diversity of tones from orange to vermilion, even on the same house, and they are generally (though not always) confined to the upper storeys. The tiles were originally applied chiefly to timber-framed buildings, where they are normally hung on horizontal oak laths, but they are now used to cover brickwork as well, in which case they are either hung on battens plugged into the walls or fixed by wooden pegs or nails into the mortar. This tile-hanging can be seen to perfection in such villages as Groombridge, near Tunbridge Wells, and Burwash, on the Forest Ridges of Sussex, but indeed it is common all over the Wealden country.

Another method of protecting the walls against the weather, applied originally to lath and plaster, but later adapted to brick as well, is by overlapping horizontal strips of wood (traditionally elm or oak, but nowadays more often pine or red cedar), called weather-boarding. The boards are generally painted white or cream on houses, though usually tarred when they are fixed on farm buildings and barns. Like tile-hanging, this attractive feature has now spread to other regions of southern England, but it is seen at its best in the Weald.

Characteristic of the houses in the Weald and Greensand country is the roofing, which is frequently designed to slope on the gable ends as well as on the front and back, and often projects down farther at the ends than in the front of the building. The impression one receives is that the village builders thought the vertical gable ends too abrupt for their dwellings. These sloping or 'hipped' roofs, as they are called, and the finely-moulded chimney-stacks also characteristic of the Wealden country are clearly not inspired by any lingering medieval tradition, and it may be suggested that village building here was in advance architecturally of that of the same period in other regions of good building in England. The straight eaves, unbroken by window openings, and the sash windows and other similar features seem to point to a Renaissance feeling when the villages of East Anglia and the Cotswolds were still influenced by their Gothic traditions.

The roof tiles, too, so abundant in Wealden villages (and usually plain tiles, not pantiles), seem to have replaced the almost universal thatch earlier than elsewhere in England. Though tiles were in use for the larger manor houses by the fourteenth century, they remained a comparative luxury and indeed were not employed extensively before the development of brickwork in the seventeenth century. Shingles, small slats of wood (oak has been ousted by Canadian cedar for these), once common over much of the country, are now to be seen principally on church spires and belfries in the south-east, where, however, they are a distinctive feature.

The use of heavy roof-slabs, made from a hard Wealden sandstone and larger and clumsier than those of the limestone belt, was a local development round Horsham that spread over the western part of the Weald, but has practically died out in recent times (I believe one quarry is still working). These slabs, or slates as they are called professionally, turn a deep brown when they are exposed, and they are used also for paving in Surrey and west Sussex. Around Petworth, still farther west in Sussex, there are many villages to which the local sandstone has contributed, especially for the lower parts of the houses; their upper parts, and notably the fine chimney-stacks, are almost all of brick, which is better suited for this purpose.

Brick, in fact, remains the predominant building material in the Weald and Greensand villages, and English brickwork is to be seen at its best here. The well-laid brick, often used artistically as well as architecturally—notably in the finely-coursed chimneys—and the neat tiles, whether on roof or walls, are features that are widespread and well-defined in the Wealden country. About the village architecture in this region, in truth, there is not only a wide and pleasing variety, but a sweet reasonableness combined with an admirable adaptability to the surroundings.

Villages of the Weald and Greensand Country

BETCHWORTH (Sy) lies in a bend of the river Mole, on the Lower Greensand, which is dominated here by the chalk escarpment of the North Downs. It remains an attractive little village, though the residential suburbs of Dorking and Reigate creep ever nearer. The best part is the road leading to the church, with seventeenth-century brick cottages on one side and old weather-boarded barns on the other. The church, its roof covered with old Horsham slabs, charmingly closes the vista.

BIDDENDEN (Kt), on the road between Tunbridge Wells and Ashford, is one of the many 'dens' or forest clearings in the eastern part of the Wealden clay. The wide village street is laid with broad flat pavements of the local Bethersden marble and has a rich variety of old houses, some timber-framed, others built of brick, some board or tile fronted, and mostly dating from the fifteenth to seventeenth centuries, when Biddenden was engaged in the flourishing cloth trade centred at Cranbrook.

BLECHINGLEY (Sy) is one of the most delightful villages on the green-sand ridge, still remarkably unspoilt though on the busy Redhill–Westerham road and within 20 miles of the centre of London. In its broad sloping street, widening as it runs downhill to the old market-place, mingle several interesting houses of various types and periods, mostly of brick and many with tile-hung upper storeys; the most noticeable is the stucco-fronted sixteenth-century inn now called the 'Whyte Harte'.

BURWASH (Sx), enchantingly situated along the highest part of one of the Forest Ridges, on the road from Lewes to Cranbrook, is one of the most charming villages of the Wealden Sands, with many fine houses lining its street, some hung with tiles, and one well-preserved brick house bearing the date 1699. Burwash in fact owes its prosperous appearance to its having been one of the most important centres of the iron industry in the fifteenth to seventeenth centuries.

CHIDDINGFOLD (Sy), on the road from Godalming to Petworth, south of the greensand heights, was the chief centre of the Wealden glass industry in the thirteenth to sixteenth centuries. The houses of this pleasant village, mostly of the seventeenth century and later, and many of them tile-hung, are set round a large irregularly-shaped green. Near the foot is the Crown Inn, with a front of decorative tiles; its structure dates from the fifteenth century, if not the fourteenth, and it claims to be the oldest licensed house in Surrey.

CHIDDINGSTONE (Kt) is a charmingly retired little village in the Vale of Eden between Edenbridge and Tonbridge. Overlooked by the tall elms secluding it from Chiddingstone Castle (the old manor house, Gothicised in the eighteenth century), it consists mainly of a fourteenth-century church, built of Wealden sandstone, and an unspoiled row of sixteenth- and seventeenth-century houses, mostly of timber with plaster or brick infillings, and including the Castle Inn, all (except the church) now fortunately in the keeping of the National Trust.

DITCHLING (Sx) is a thriving village on a rise of the Lower Greensand dominated by Ditchling Beacon, one of the highest points of the South Downs. Though perhaps too easily reached from Brighton for safety, it still retains some delightful old buildings in its main street, especially Anne of Cleves' House, a rambling early-sixteenth-century mansion of brick and half-timberwork, with projecting gables, a carved verge-board and a curious outside flight of steps. It stands opposite the church, whose central tower has a pyramidal cap peculiar to Sussex.

GOUDHURST (Kt) is a village of entrancing irregularity pitched on the crest and slope of a steep hill climbed by the road from Tunbridge Wells to Ashford. It has a well-restored fifteenth-century timber-framed inn, the Star and Eagle, and many fine small houses of the sixteenth and seventeenth centuries which are being preserved for the National Trust. The village shows up extremely well from a distance, and itself commands an extensive view over the rich woodlands and orchards of perhaps the loveliest part of the Weald.

GROOMBRIDGE (Kt), on the road from Tunbridge Wells to East Grinstead, is a pleasing little village the older part of which is grouped round a triangular tree-shaded green on a steep slope above a tributary of the Medway. At the upper end of the green is a brick-paved walk with a row of cottages that is, rather unusually, both tile-hung and weather-boarded. Close by the excellent brick church of 1625 is the entrance to Groombridge Place, a charming moated manor house of the seventeenth century, also in brick.

IGHTHAM (Kt) is on the Sevenoaks–Maidstone road below the escarpment of the North Downs. It has an unusually attractive group of fifteenth- to sixteenth-century timber-framed houses that includes the Town House (now an hotel) and the George and Dragon Inn, nestling picturesquely in a hollow. The interesting twelfth- to fifteenth-century church stands aloof, on a knoll surrounded by orchards; the road past it leads to Ightham Court, a house of 1575 with fine trees and shrubs in its garden.

LAMBERHURST (Kt), though situated on the main London to Hastings road, still retains its old-world atmosphere. It lies in the pleasant valley of the little river Teise, and cottages with weather-boarded and tiled fronts line the village street. Coggins Hall, nearly opposite the George and Dragon Inn, is a fine timber-framed house of the Tudor period. Lamberhurst was a flourishing centre of the Wealden iron industry, the last furnace of which was blown out about 1830.

LINDFIELD (Sx) remains one of the most delightful villages of the Weald, though now on the edge of the much-favoured 'commuter' country whose centre is Hayward's Heath. Its many lovely houses of the sixteenth to eighteenth centuries, some with timber-framing, some with thatched or stone-tiled roofs, are mainly gathered round the church, which is chiefly of the thirteenth and fourteenth centuries. Below this is a pleasant green with a pond, an unusual feature in the Weald.

LINGFIELD (Sy), to the east of the London–Eastbourne road, is one of the pleasantest villages of the Wealden clay, though rather too scattered and a little too suburbanised. It has several picturesque groups of houses, however, the best in the road leading to the church. They include the former Star Inn, of about 1700 (a brick building restored as the church house), and the fifteenth- to sixteenth-century timber-framed house opposite, incorporating a rare feature in its contemporary shop front.

MAYFIELD (Sx), on the road from Tunbridge Wells to Eastbourne, is one of the most enchanting villages of the Wealden Sands, re-markably situated on the end of an almost detached ridge. Among the many attractive old buildings in its long street are the Middle House Hotel, timber-framed and bearing the date 1575, and another timbered house dated 1420, and at the foot of the street is the Lower House, a timber-framed Jacobean building. Near the church are the fourteenth-century remains of a palace of the Archbishops of Canterbury.

NORTHIAM (Sx), on the road from Hastings to Tenterden, is a high-lying village with a variety of old houses. Hayes Farm (now an hotel), near the green, is partly of the sixteenth century, partly of the eighteenth, and on the green itself is Queen Elizabeth's Oak, under which that monarch dined during a progress to Rye. The church, close by, built largely of ironstone from the Weald, has a tall spire, unusual for Sussex, of the early sixteenth century. The great house of Brickwall, farther south, has an ornate timber-framed façade of the seventeenth century.

OTHAM (Kt), on the side of a valley south of the Maidstone–Ashford road, is one of the most pleasantly secluded villages of the Wealden clay. Embowered in orchards and hop-gardens, it enjoys enticing views of the North Downs and has many fine fifteenth- to seventeenth-century timber-framed houses in its long street. Stoneacre, in a steep lane east of the street, is an exceptionally fine and well-restored yeoman's house of the fifteenth century, now the property of the National Trust.

PENSHURST (Kt) is a charming small village in a pleasant valley at the junction of the Eden with the Medway, dominated by the great house of Penshurst Place, a delightfully mellowed mixture of red brick and stone, mainly Elizabethan, the historic seat of the Sidneys since 1552. The house is approached through the churchyard, and this is reached through an opening beneath one of a picturesque group of late-fifteenth-century timber-framed cottages which has, very unusually, an infilling of oak boarding.

SEDLESCOMBE (Sx), perhaps the most delightful village in the eastern part of the Weald, was a thriving centre of the ironworking industry in the sixteenth and seventeenth centuries. Attractive houses of this period line the long green threaded by the Hastings–Maidstone road as this ascends from the river Brede, and the village has also a restored fifteenth-century inn, the Queen's Head. The first Pestalozzi village in Britain for displaced and needy children of all nations was opened at Sedlescombe in 1958.

SHERE (Sy), generally claimed to be the prettiest village in the county, had the misfortune to be on the busy Dorking–Guildford road until a new by-pass was completed in 1960. Shere is charmingly situated in the finely-wooded valley of the Tillingbourne immediately below the steep escarpment of the North Downs, and its most attractive part, with sixteenth- to seventeenth-century houses, some of them timber-framed, is off the main road, beyond the little river and on the way to the church.

SUTTON VALENCE (Kt) is on the comparatively quiet Maidstone–Tenterden road where this crosses the ridge of the Quarry Hills, as that part of the greensand range to the south of Maidstone is called. The pleasing village is spread out along two 'terraces' on the sharp slope of the escarpment and commands a wonderful view over miles and miles of the 'dim blue goodness of the Weald'. It

took the second part of its name from the Valences, originally a
Norman family, of whose small early medieval castle there are a
few remains east of the village.

WEST HOATHLY (Sx), in quiet country west of the London–Lewes
road, is an attractive hill-top village, one of the few of very old
foundation on the Wealden ridges (all of them on the tops of hills),
and enjoys a wide prospect all round. Opposite the church is the
Elizabethan stone manor house, carefully restored, and in the road
leading south is the old priest's house, a fine fifteenth-century
timber-framed building now containing a fascinating collection of
Sussex domestic 'bygones'.

WITLEY (Sy), strung out along the Godalming–Petworth road, is one of
the most engaging villages on the Lower Greensand, with picturesque groups of building here and there. At the top of the hill is
a row of timber-framed houses, and the brick-and-tile White
Hart, farther south, is a most charming inn. The timber-framed
cottages in the lane opposite, at the foot of the steps to the churchyard, have their upper storeys covered with tiles of a 'fish-tail'
pattern (see the illustration of Witley) characteristic of the Weald
and Greensand Country.

2 The Chalk Country

The chalkland which is certainly the best-known landscape feature of
the south-east half of England stretches right across the country from
Dorset to Norfolk and includes Salisbury Plain, the Berkshire Downs
and the Chiltern Hills. Less prominent in East Anglia (which in any
case has an individuality that demands separate consideration), it is
continued beyond the Wash by the Lincolnshire Wolds and again
beyond the Humber by the Yorkshire Wolds, a range that ends
distinctively in Flamborough Head.

From the central plateau of Wiltshire and Hampshire, the hub of
southern England from prehistoric times onward, the chalk pushes out
two long arms eastward as the North and South Downs, enclosing the
Weald and Greensand Country. (The way these downs were formed is
described in the previous section.) The North Downs, the 'backbone
of Kent and Surrey', are broken off seaward in the famous white
cliffs of Dover; the South Downs, the 'bold, majestic downs, smooth,

fair and lonely' of the poet Robert Bridges, end similarly in the stately cliffs of Beachy Head and the Seven Sisters. More than anything else, it is these abrupt terminations, facing travellers returning across the Channel, that have marked the downland as being expressive of the English scene.

The North Downs have an outlier in the promontory of the Isle of Thanet, culminating in the North Foreland, while another belt of chalk stretches across the Isle of Wight to end in the jagged Needles at the entrance to The Solent. Beyond this strait, the range is extended across Dorset from Swanage as the Purbeck Hills. The main mass of chalkland from Dorset to the South Downs of Sussex encloses a large bay of clays of more recent formation which includes the northern half of the Isle of Wight, the New Forest and the country on both sides of Southampton Water, and is usually called the Hampshire Basin. Rural building here follows much the same pattern as in the other clay areas, but the distribution of the villages is noticeably irregular. There are great tracts of open or wooded country like Beaulieu Heath and the New Forest around Lyndhurst, and few settlements could be seen in this district until quite recent times. Though it has some very attractive scenery, the Hampshire Basin is 'unrewarding' to the seeker after villages, and I have thought best to deal with it in this section rather than with the other clay country from which it is separated.

The great chalk belt from Dorset to Norfolk is almost broken through by the valley of the Kennet and its extension westward, the Vale of Pewsey. These, not the Thames, form the natural link from east to west in the passage from the Thames valley to the Bristol Channel. The Kennet, as can be seen from the map, prolongs the line of the lower Thames due west, and the gap made by the Thames itself in the chalk, between the Berkshire Downs and the Chilterns, is geologically unimportant. In view of this, and also because the chalk covers such a vast area, I have divided my villages into three sub-sections: (a) the North and South Downs; (b) the chalklands south of the Kennet, including Salisbury Plain and the Hampshire and Dorset heights, as well as the Isle of Wight and the Hampshire Basin; and (c) the chalklands north of the Kennet, principally the Berkshire Downs and the Chilterns. For reasons I have already explained, I have included the Lincolnshire Wolds with the Fens and Lincolnshire as a whole (Section 5), and the wolds of the East Riding with the country east of the Pennines (Section 12).

The chalklands display a great variation, not only in their formation, but in their soil and vegetation, and this has had a marked effect on village building. To deal with the formation first: the North and South Downs have long, steep escarpments on the sides facing the Weald, interrupted only where some river forces a passage through on its way towards the Thames or the sea. From the level crests of the escarpments, the dip slopes descend gradually outward as undulating plateaux. The Chiltern Hills and to some extent the Berkshire Downs have a similar formation; the Chilterns are in effect the reverse face of the North Downs, the London Basin (Section 3) filling the dip between them.

As the chalk approaches East Anglia it begins to lose its character. There are no definite ranges of hills here, and eastward the surface is covered by a wide bed of drift clay left by the retreating glaciers at the end of the Ice Age. The chalklands merge without any distinctive boundary into the lowlands of East Anglia, with which indeed they share the style of their village architecture.

Village settlement was greatly influenced by the natural conditions underfoot. Much of the chalk, for example, has a superficial covering of clay intermixed with flints—nodules of a hard quartz, usually black or dark grey when freshly dug, but developing a white crust after exposure. Where this covering occurs (and the grass here is noticeably different from the close turf of the chalk itself), it was possible to work the land more readily; it was on these chalklands, in fact, that the earliest settlers found their best opportunities for cultivation. Where the chalk is covered with a clay cap, high-lying villages may be seen in fair numbers. Some of the oldest settlements, such as the original village of Coulsdon, in Surrey, first mentioned in 675, are to be found here. Where the land is comparatively low, too, the chalk has a covering of more fertile soil and villages are distributed with some regularity.

But on the open uncapped chalkland itself, especially where the land is higher and the conditions naturally rather bleaker, villages of any size are few and far between. The absence of water and of timber for building or shelter were other factors militating against any large settlement on the downs. Though prehistoric man had eked out his miserable existence on the heights, the Saxons mostly preferred to ignore the uncapped chalklands as an area of settlement. They began to cultivate the valley bottoms which had not been accessible in earlier times, and they built their villages in the valleys, where they had plenty of timber and access to water from a stream or from the springs that issue at the foot of the permeable chalk. On the South Downs, for instance, settlements of any size (not counting, of course, the egregious modern developments) are few, the villages being mainly confined to the valleys by which the rivers push their way through the downs, though others have grown up on the narrow strip of the Upper Greensand that runs as a terrace below the face of the escarpment.

The villages of the chalk country as a whole are mostly dispersed at the base of the escarpments or along the many valleys that break through the chalk. Strings of small villages, in the main as yet un-spoiled, are typical of the Dorset downs, the valleys running up into Salisbury Plain, and the Berkshire Downs. They could be built close together, as they had the advantage not only of the rich soil of the valley meadowlands, but of long strips of the high pasture on the uplands stretching out on either side of the valley.

Despite all the variations in the formation and texture of the chalk-lands, there are features in the villages which are noticeable throughout the whole of the belt from Dorset to East Anglia and from Wiltshire to Kent and Sussex, in contrast with those of the clay and other lands that surround the chalk. In the south especially, the villages show an attractive and distinctive type of building. The older houses on the open chalk, particularly where timber was difficult to obtain, were frequently of cob—a substance we shall meet with again in Devon (page 144)—raised on a foundation of rubble or flint. But as standards in village building improved, flint was introduced into the walls; in Kent, for instance, there are many small and secluded villages with cottages built entirely of flint, and it is the common building material on the chalklands of Hampshire and Berkshire.

Flint had of course been used by itself since the time of the Romans, and can be seen in many of the surviving fortifications of those in-vaders. But the strength of a flint building depends on the quality of the mortar employed (the Roman mortar must have been good to have lasted). If the flints are large or of particularly irregular shape, a great

deal of mortar is required. So, where possible, the flint was bonded
with stone or brick to make it stronger—stone where it was readily
obtainable from the greensand or from the limestone belt approaching
the chalk on the west; brick where the chalk bordered the clay lands to
the east. In the larger houses, the external angles were often dressed
with stone or brick quoins, and the combination of flints with squares
of stone to make a chequer pattern became a favourite form of
decoration. There are many examples of this among the Wiltshire downs, but in some of the smaller houses here the walls are
made of soft chalk which has been 'pugged' by adding water,
then poured between boards and rammed down and left to dry before
it is used.

In Dorset and Wiltshire, especially in such valleys as that of the
Wylye, there are many examples of simple domestic building in
which flint has been used in conjunction with sandstone or the oolitic
limestone with a very satisfying effect. On the slopes of the Chilterns,
and to a lesser extent the North Downs, both regions where the supply
of wood was abundant, timber-framed cottages with an infilling of
flint or brick nogging are more common. From Hertfordshire northward, where good nodules of flint are generally harder to come by,
only the older houses incorporate flint, the newer ones are of a light-
toned brick made from the gault clay found (as in the Weald) at the
foot of the chalk.

Thatch from corn straw or (less frequently) Norfolk reed was once
the automatic choice for roofing material in the chalklands, though
the hipped roofs, like the weather-boarding, to be seen here and there
below the South Downs show the influence of the Weald. Thatched
roofs predominated everywhere in the chalk country until comparatively recent years, but thatching is unhappily a dying art in many
parts of England; roofs of the ubiquitous slate and the red tile, cheaper
to build and easier to repair, are ousting the natural materials. We now
see fewer of those heavy overhanging roofs cut by the easy curves of the
upper windows which convey a genuine picture of old England,
or indeed of the white plaster that goes so well with them.
About such dwellings there is still a feeling for landscape as
well as a natural modesty in keeping with the simple lives of
the villagers of the chalklands described by Thomas Hardy and
W. H. Hudson.

Villages of the Chalk Country

(a) *The North and South Downs:*

ALFRISTON (Sx) stands near the entrance to the gap by which the
Cuckmere River penetrates the South Downs, its houses, embowered in trees, making a delightful picture as seen from the
surrounding heights. The several timber-framed buildings include
the charming Star Inn, established in the thirteenth century by the
monks of Battle Abbey as a hostel for pilgrims; the present building,
largely of the fifteenth century, has a roof of massive Horsham
slabs. Near the church is the lovely thatched and timber-framed
Clergy House, built about 1350.

AMBERLEY (Sx), on a terrace below the South Downs at the north end
of the gap made by the river Arun, overlooks the Amberley Wild
Brooks (i.e. 'Weald Brooks'), probably a lake in medieval times.
It is a village of fascinating irregularity, with many attractive old
cottages tucked away, some of them having thatched roofs, and the
pleasant remains of a fourteenth-century fortified manor house of
the bishops of Chichester.

AYLESFORD (Kt) is actually on the Medway between the greensand and
the North Downs, but is dominated by the chalk escarpment. The
medieval pilgrims must have crossed the river here, by its lowest
ford, on their way to the shrine of St Thomas Becket at Canterbury.
The bridge is partly of the fourteenth century; above it are
picturesque houses, timber-framed and red tiled, backed by the
church on its high bank and a line of lofty elms.

BRAMBER (Sx), under the South Downs, near the entrance to the Adur
gap, consists mainly of one long street, at the east end of which is
the beautiful timber-framed house of St Mary's, dating mainly
from the fifteenth to sixteenth centuries. The church, on the
steep hillside above the west end of the village, was originally built
about 1075 as the chapel of Bramber Castle, of which there are
some remains higher up, on an isolated chalk mound commanding
the Wealden clay.

CHILHAM (Kt), perhaps the most satisfying village of the North Downs,
is placed on the end of a steep-sided ridge, between the roads from
Canterbury to Maidstone and Hastings, but thickly screened by
trees. Its broad square is enclosed by well-preserved sixteenth-

century timber-framed and later brick houses, overlooked on one side by the church, which has a fifteenth-century tower of chequered flint and stone, on the other by the gates of the seventeenth-century Chilham Castle, the beautiful grounds of which were laid out by 'Capability' Brown.

ELHAM (Kt), in the quiet valley of the Little Stour, between Folkestone and Canterbury, has some fine sixteenth- to seventeenth-century timber-framed houses in its long main street, their overhanging upper storeys carrying quaintly-carved brackets that support the heavy eaves. Just off the street, by contrast, is a secluded little market square with red-brick houses of the eighteenth century.

LENHAM (Kt), below the long wooded escarpment of the North Downs, is now fortunately avoided by the Maidstone–Canterbury road. The village flourished as an important market during the eighteenth century, and its market house, encased in brick and now converted into shops, still stands in the spacious and old-fashioned market place, on the north side of which, screened by lime trees, is a row of houses of curiously Continental aspect. The church, full of interesting details, is reached through a fifteenth-century lich-gate.

SOUTH HARTING (Sx) is a delightful village charmingly situated below the wooded face of the South Downs, near the Hampshire border. It has some eighteenth-century houses with red-brick and cream-washed fronts in its broad main street. This slopes up towards the church, which has a spire, rebuilt in 1936, reaching 130 feet above the ground and sheathed, rather unusually, in copper. Outside the churchyard wall are preserved the old parish stocks and whipping-post.

STEYNING (Sx) stands near the northern entrance to the Adur gap. A port of some importance until its harbour in the river silted up, it is now an enchanting village wearing an air of antiquity and serenity, and with many fine eighteenth-century brick houses and others of timber-framed construction. In the main street is the Old Market House, with a quaint clock-tower and belfry, and in Church Street the Old Grammar School, occupying the buildings of a fourteenth-century brotherhood. The church, one of the most beautiful in Sussex, is the surviving part of a larger and noble Norman structure.

TELSCOMBE (Sx) is a charming little village secluded among trees in a fold of the South Downs above the valley of the Ouse, still unspoilt though almost overshadowed by the bungalow growths of Saltdean and Peacehaven and at no great distance from Brighton. The luxuriance of the trees enclosing the little Norman church and quiet cottages seems all the richer in contrast with the bareness of the downs around them.

WEST DEAN (Sx), which lies north of the Eastbourne–Seaford road in a little tributary glen running up from the Cuckmere valley, is a delightful village enfolded by the swelling downs and hidden from the outside world by tall elms and beeches. Its mellow and flowery cottages are built of flint in the best and most characteristic downland style, as is the thirteenth- to fifteenth-century church, to the south-east of which is an old pigeon house.

(b) The Chalklands South of the Kennet, with the Hampshire Basin

BEAULIEU (Hp) is delightfully positioned on the borders of the New Forest, at the head of the long tidal inlet of the Beaulieu River, which runs up from The Solent. Consisting almost wholly of one street, its houses built of brick with plain tiled roofs, it is best approached by the road from Southampton, rounding the headwaters of the creek and passing the entrance to the parish church and other remains of the powerful Cistercian house of Beaulieu Abbey, founded in 1204.

BOSHAM (Sx), a fishing village and yachting centre on an arm of Chichester Harbour, is an exceptionally charming and historic place. Quay Meadow, from which Harold II set out on his unfortunate excursion to Normandy in 1064, is a pleasant greensward in the angle between two creeks, and close by is the church, with a Saxon tower and other work of the period represented in conventional fashion on the Bayeux Tapestry that records the voyage.

CERNE ABBAS (Dt) is beautifully situated deep in the valley by which the Dorchester–Sherborne road penetrates the chalk hills of Dorset. The best of its well-preserved sixteenth-century timbered houses, with projecting upper storeys, are in the road leading past the noble fifteenth-century church. Parts of the Benedictine abbey survive in the Abbey House, with its stone and flint gables, and the fifteenth-century gatehouse, which has a carved oriel window. Cut in the chalk slopes above the village is the remarkable figure of the Cerne Giant, believed to be of Romano-British origin.

CHILMARK (Wt), between the Wylye and Nadder valleys south of the road from Salisbury to Wincanton, is famous for the oolite quarries, now disused, from which the stone for Salisbury Cathedral was taken. It lies in a little valley protected on the north by a range of rolling downs partly clad with beech woods. The main street follows the course of the stream, with the church spire rising in the background, and stone is used everywhere with the prodigality possible in a former quarrying village.

CORFE CASTLE (Dt), or just Corfe, if you wish, is a fascinating village sheltered by the line of downs which runs across the bold promontory of the Isle of Purbeck. Above it, on an isolated conical hill, rise the gaunt Norman ruins of the castle built to protect a gap in the downs. The houses of the village, like the castle, are of silver-grey limestone from the near-by Purbeck outcrop and they have heavy stone-slab roofs and door sills. The old-world Greyhound Inn (one of the few buildings with a cream-washed front) and several other houses in the village have remarkable projecting porticos supported by pillars.

EAST LULWORTH (Dt), a little inland from the chalk cliffs of the Isle of Purbeck and the curious circular formation of Lulworth Cove, is a very pleasant village in a wooded hollow. Its thatched cottages and flowery gardens are scattered around the park walls of the early-seventeenth-century Lulworth Castle, a square feudal-looking mansion with round towers at the angles. Here is 'metely good ground, and plenty of wood', in the words of Leland, the sixteenth-century traveller.

GODSHILL (IW) is a very pretty village under Appuldurcombe Down, on the road from Shanklin to Newport, its thatched and stone-built houses overlooked by the tower of its fifteenth-century church. In some of the houses the thatch is carried down to form a canopy over the door. Godshill's only disadvantage is that it is within easy reach of Sandown, Ventnor and other Isle of Wight resorts, and consequently tends to be rather too popular, like many well-known villages, during the summer season. At other times it is of course delightful.

14 *South Harting, Sussex*

MELBURY OSMUND (Dt) is a delectable little village hidden away in a valley west of the Dorchester–Yeovil road, below the northern slopes of the Dorset chalklands and at the edge of the large Melbury Park. Only the eighteenth-century church tower on its hill can be seen outside the valley; the two rows of grey stone cottages that make up most of the village are in the lane that leads down from the open space shaded by dark yews at the churchyard gates to the stream at the bottom.

MILTON ABBAS (Dt), among the peaceful downs some distance north of the Dorchester–Salisbury road, is a planned village created about 1786 by the first Earl of Dorchester, who pulled down the old village when he built himself an imposing mansion beside the ruined church of Milton Abbey. Spaced on either side of the greens bordering the road descending the valley are pairs of thatched-roofed cottages, all of identical design, with the contemporary church in the centre. Though the chestnuts planted between the houses have mostly been felled, the village, enclosed by woodlands, retains its atmosphere of seclusion and serenity.

NETHER WALLOP (Hp), a quietly attractive village north of the main London–Salisbury road, lies in a tributary valley of the Avon, surrounded by the spreading downs. Trees seem to have sprung up everywhere, and the cottages, many of which are thatched, are arranged in no sort of order—a typical fragmented village, in fact. Some of the cottages have their walls built up of alternate bands of brick and flint, an arrangement peculiar to this district.

SELBORNE (Hp), between the roads from London to Gosport and Portsmouth, but fortunately far enough removed from both, has a setting worthy of the great eighteenth-century naturalist who made it famous. Gilbert White lived at The Wakes (since enlarged), opposite the pleasant green set off the main street and leading to the church, and he is buried in the churchyard. By the church door is an ancient yew. The village nestles under the great hanging beechwood on Selborne Hill which is still its chief glory, as in Gilbert White's day.

SHORWELL (IW), the most delightful village in the Isle of Wight, enjoys a sheltered position at the foot of a combe running into the downs that stretch right across the island. It lies mostly just off the main road from Ventnor to Freshwater, and the lovely stone-

15 *Bosham, Sussex*

built and thatched cottages are grouped about the interesting fifteenth-century church. North Court, in beautifully wooded grounds north of the church, was built in 1615; West Court is a sixteenth- to seventeenth-century house.

SOUTHWICK (Hp) is on the Portsmouth–Winchester road and the north side of Portsdown Hill, a long narrow ridge of chalk that overlooks Portsmouth Harbour in the other direction. The village has a broad street lined with attractive warm-coloured cottages leading up to the pleasant little flint and stone church, of the fourteenth and sixteenth centuries, outside the long lines of brick wall that surround the park of Southwick House.

(c) The Chalklands North of the Kennet, including the Chilterns:

ALDBOURNE (Wt), a centre of racehorse training on the Hungerford–Swindon road, is a real village of the downs, with an interesting plan. Approaching from the south, the road bends round the village pond, then unexpectedly opens up a wide green, from which an easy slope, grouped round with brick and colour-washed cottages, leads up to the fine church set high above the roofs of the houses, the whole forming a pleasing and dignified composition.

ALDBURY (Ht) lies north of the London–Aylesbury road, below the beautifully wooded downs that run out from Ashridge to Ivinghoe Beacon. The centre of this very attractive Chiltern village is the large triangular green, which has a pond sheltered by a fine elm tree, with the ancient stocks close by. On two sides are charming sixteenth- to seventeenth-century timber-framed houses, while the church, which is mostly of the thirteenth to fifteenth centuries, stands off to the south-west.

ASHWELL (Ht) is in the extreme north of the Hertfordshire chalklands, between the roads from Baldock to Biggleswade and Royston. The fifteenth-century Guildhall of St John, with its closely-spaced timber uprights, and the gabled sixteenth-century Town House (now a museum) are two of the several well-preserved houses in the delightful main street. The splendid tower and slim spire, 176 feet high, of the excellent fourteenth-century church stand out over the great fields which surround the village.

AVEBURY (Wt), on the head-waters of the Kennet near the Swindon–Devizes road, is unique in being enclosed by the massive rampart and ditch and megalithic circle of Sarsens, 'perhaps the most important Early Bronze Age monument in Europe'. But in addition to this, the village has a Saxon church with Norman and later additions, and a fine Elizabethan manor house with unusual topiary gardens and with stables which now contain a museum of relics from the Avebury circle. The stables, like many of the houses in the village, are built with Sarsens, which are sandstone boulders from the downs.

BRADENHAM (Bu), just off the road which runs through a Chiltern valley between High Wycombe and Princes Risborough, is dominated by its church, which has a fifteenth-century grey flint tower, and its great red-brick manor house of the late seventeenth century, long the home of Isaac D'Israeli, the father of Lord Beaconsfield. Almost the whole of the pretty village, with its trim cottages facing the spacious green, and the surrounding farms and beechwoods are in the hands of the National Trust.

EAST HAGBOURNE (Bk) is an exceptionally picturesque village below the escarpment of the Berkshire Downs, between the roads from Wantage to Reading and Wallingford, and perhaps rather too near the modern spate of building around Didcot Junction for full enjoyment. The interesting fourteenth- to fifteenth-century church with its timber-framed porches and handsome tower, however, the restored fifteenth-century cross and the charming seventeenth- to eighteenth-century cottages of brick and timber compose a picture characteristic of the English village at its best.

EAST HENDRED (Bk), just off the Wantage–Reading road, under the chalk escarpment, is now too close to the sprawling Nuclear Research Establishment at Harwell for comfort. But it is a characteristically charming village with thatched and timber-framed cottages of the sixteenth and seventeenth centuries, an unusual fifteenth-century wayside chapel with a priest's house adjoining, and a church with a stately fifteenth-century tower. Hendred House has been the property of the Eyston family since 1450.

FINGEST (Bu) is in the delightfully-wooded Chilterns, near the head of a long valley running up from the Henley–Marlow road which follows the north bank of the Thames. An exceptionally secluded small village, it has pleasant timber-framed and eighteenth-century brick houses gathered round its Norman church, the chief feature of which is the unusually large tower, with unique twin gables supporting a saddleback roof, perhaps of the seventeenth century.

HAMBLEDEN (Bu), a long way down the valley from Fingest, nearer the Henley–Marlow road, is a very attractive village mostly grouped round a triangular green. On one side of this is the church (its tower was heightened and encased in the local flint in 1883) and along the others are typical brick or flint and brick cottages, above the roofs of which rise the gables of the late-seventeenth-century manor house, also of flint and red brick. The rectory, built in 1724 of brick, stands outside the village.

STEVENTON (Bk), on the lower slopes of the downland escarpment, lies mostly to the west of the busy Oxford–Winchester road. This delightful village has a long green traversed by a raised paved causeway shaded by old elms and skirted by some lovely gabled timber-framed seventeenth-century cottages with fine brick chimneys. One house has parget plaster work (see page 98) and another is dated 1657. Priory Cottages, west of the railway, incorporates the great hall of the former monastic buildings here.

WENDOVER (Bu), on the Amersham–Aylesbury road, almost closes the gap in the Chilterns between the wooded heights of Boddington Hill and Coombe Hill. It is practically a little town, but it has many exceptionally attractive houses of the eighteenth century, most of which are brick fronted, though some have timber-framing with an infilling of white plaster and occasionally flint. The best of the houses are in the High Street and (especially) the wide Aylesbury road, where they form two unbroken rows.

WEST WYCOMBE (Bu), though on the eternally busy main road from London to Oxford, remains an unspoilt village, thanks to its preservation by the National Trust. The fronts of the houses, some of the fifteenth to sixteenth centuries, but more of the seventeenth and eighteenth, show a mingling of brick and plasterwork, and timber-framing with brick and plaster infilling. The village is overlooked on the north by an eighteenth-century 'classical' church (its tower surmounted by a curious ball), built by Sir Francis Dashwood, founder of the so-called 'Hell-Fire' Club, and by his prominent flint-built mausoleum of 1764. On the

16 *West Wycombe, Buckinghamshire*

south side of the village are the ornamental grounds of West Wycombe Park, a house remodelled by Sir Francis about 1765.

3 The Clay Country

The chalk which covers a great part of south-east England and forms its most prominent geological feature is overlaid in places by wide tracts of more recent deposits. These consist chiefly of clays and sands laid down under marine conditions, and the most familiar of them is responsible for the structure of the lower valley of the Thames. The earth movements which pushed up the North Downs on the one hand and the Chilterns on the other naturally created the dip between them, and the deposits laid down in this basin were so soft that they were readily worn away to form a wide shallow valley by the rivers flowing east towards the North Sea.

This region, often called the London Basin, includes not only the valley of the Thames up to the gorge by which the river forces its way through the chalk, but that of its tributary and natural extension westward, the Kennet (to beyond Newbury), as well as both shores of the Thames estuary. The clay also extends north-east over Essex and Suffolk to the flat coastline as far as the Orwell estuary, but the villages of the northern part of Essex take on the East Anglian character of Norfolk and Suffolk, and I have thought it more logical to consider them in that section.

The basin of the lower Thames, then, is an area of low ground enclosed on every side except the sea by the higher land of the chalk. It must not be thought that this makes the scenery dull, or the villages everywhere uninteresting. The centre of the basin, it is true, is occupied by the capital and the grasping tentacles of its suburbs, which reach out and clasp ever more and more of those once quiet agricultural villages which not so long ago stood well out in the country. Other villages are losing their souls, too, by becoming the centres of 'commuter country' (horrible expression!) The great rush to the towns which started with the Industrial Revolution, and has gained momentum ever since, is now being offset by a rush the other way on the part of townworkers eager to live in the country. But outside the swelling mass of suburbia and the areas of desirable modern residences, a considerable variety of quiet scenery is still to be found by those who

17 *Milton Abbas, Dorset*

seek it: the lush green meadows bordering the Thames, where 'the silent river glides by flowering banks'—no longer silent, I am afraid, in some reaches in high summer, especially at week-ends—the quiet homely pastures that still make up a great deal of Hertfordshire and Essex, and the dry sandy heathlands of north Surrey and Berkshire, along the northern margin of the chalk.

The London Clay on which most of the metropolis is built is basically a thick, dark brown or grey deposit, extending as a belt across the counties bordering the Thames and along the north coast of Kent to the Medway. The London Basin is not one continuous unrelieved splodge of clay, however. Underneath it lies a series of gravelly beds—various kinds of clays and sands mixed with harder flints and pebbles—and where these break through to the surface they are often shaped into low hills, as they are at Highgate, Hampstead and Harrow on the north side of London, and Wimbledon and Blackheath on the south. I mention these places not only because they are familiar to Londoners, but also because each of them retains (in however modified a form) the nucleus of an old village whose origins pre-date those of many on the clay itself.

Among the several belts of the gravelly formations are the Thanet Sands, which (as we might guess from their name) stretch eastward to the coast of Kent. The towns and villages on the road from Guildford to Croydon likewise lie along a narrow outcrop of the Thanet Sands at the foot of the chalk slopes of the North Downs, and they mostly originated as settlements round the springs where the water which seeps through the permeable chalk comes to the surface. Between Epsom and Croydon are a succession of places—Ewell, Cheam, Sutton, Carshalton and Beddington—which have all grown into dormitory towns serving the needs of the capital and are now joined to one another, but among all the modern housing will be found several survivals of old-world villages. Carshalton, for example, still retains a charming weather-boarded inn, the Greyhound, and other eighteenth-century buildings grouped round its ponds. But in general, I must say, the 'lost villages' of outer London (and other great cities) only serve as a grim warning of what is happening increasingly to our countryside.

On top of the London Clay were deposited later gravels, one of which, the Bagshot Sands, takes its name from a considerable outcrop in north-west Surrey. The scenery of these once-lonely heathlands is attractive, but this has long been favourite 'commuter country' and the villages have suffered (as they always do) in consequence of their being suburbanised.

The whole region of the clay country was formerly well wooded, but as the timber was cleared the land was given over to pasture. On the heavy and intractable soil of the clay itself, relatively few settlements were established; they were mostly confined to the sandy and gravelly beds. The claylands are deficient, of course, in what has always been the finest building material in England—stone. Grey sandstone boulders from Bagshot Heath were used to face Windsor Castle as early as the twelfth century, but until the coming of the railways, stone was much too expensive to transport for almost everything but the larger buildings, unless it could be carried by water. In its place, the villager used what he had always used successfully—his native materials.

Flint was employed to some extent in the districts nearest the chalklands, though the villages of the Thames and Kennet valleys show surprisingly little of the chalk that encloses them. In Hertfordshire, where the clay country merges into the chalk, flint was used extensively for churches and the larger houses; small houses were often built of 'clunch', hard blocks of solid chalk, usually quarried from under the surface chalk. But the main materials were timber, while it was plentiful, with plaster and thatch, and later brick. Many timber-framed cottages of the sixteenth century (some perhaps even of the fifteenth; it is hard to tell) have survived in the clay country, but timber was employed decreasingly as the woodlands were thinned out. From the seventeenth century, at least, it was used only in conjunction with brick, and timber-framed houses with an infilling of brick nogging are characteristic. But since the eighteenth century, the chief material for village building in the claylands has been brick itself, for which the large deposits of clay and sand were admirably suited.

In those areas of Essex covered by the clay, bricks have been made since the thirteenth century, though it was not until the fifteenth century that they were employed to any great extent, and even then they were used only in the larger houses and occasionally for church building. Essex has about thirty towers, dating from the fifteenth to the early seventeenth century, completely of brick (large and magnificent some of them are) and at least 15 churches are adorned with brick porches. This is especially remarkable when it is realised that brick was not used for churches elsewhere until the last century or so, even in those areas entirely without stone.

The clay regions of Essex were covered by a great forest in the Middle Ages, and even later were more heavily wooded than most regions. In consequence timber has been employed in the churches here much more than elsewhere. An unusual number of churches have timber porches, mostly of the fourteenth and fifteenth centuries, but yet more remarkable are the timber towers and steeples, of which those at Blackmore, Navestock and Margaretting (the lower stage here has a rarity in its vertical weather-boarding) deserve special mention; none seem to date earlier than the fifteenth century. In Greenstead, too, as I mentioned before, Essex has the only surviving example in England of a Saxon timber church. Among domestic building, the claylands of Essex are particularly rich in timber-framed farmhouses and barns, many of them belonging to the fifteenth and sixteenth centuries. The weather-boarding with which we became familiar in the Weald and Greensand Country is also frequently to be seen here.

Villages of the Clay Country

ALDERMASTON (Bk), in the Kennet valley between Reading and Newbury, now seems fated to be associated in the popular mind with research into atomic weapons. The establishment for this is fortunately at some distance from the village, which remains a quietly attractive place, its street of mellow brick and tile seventeenth- to eighteenth-century cottages climbing the slope from the white-fronted Hind's Head Hotel to the seventeenth-century lodges, with their Flemish gables, of Aldermaston Court, at the top of the hill.

BRAY (Bk) is a pleasant village and favourite boating resort on the south bank of the Thames between Maidenhead and Windsor. Near the river is the much-restored church, which has a handsome fifteenth-century tower and contains the grave of Simon Aleyn, the famous turncoat vicar. The churchyard is entered through a lich-gate under the church house. At the south end of the village are the picturesque early-seventeenth-century red-brick alms-houses of Jesus Hospital, enclosing a quadrangle with a garden.

COBHAM (Kt) is a delightful village on the northern edge of the chalk, outside the park of the Elizabethan Cobham Hall and south of the Dartford–Rochester road. Behind the church, a fine thirteenth- to fourteenth-century building famous for its brasses, are the College Almshouses, refounded in 1598, and opposite is the timber-framed Leather Bottle Inn, the 'clean and commodious ale-house' where the love-lorn Mr Tracy Tupman stayed in *Pickwick Papers*. At the west end of the village, which also has some excellent weather-boarded cottages of the early nineteenth century, is the fine seventeenth-century brick house of Owletts.

DENHAM (Bu), on the Misbourne, a tributary of the Colne, north of the London–Oxford road, is now only just beyond the fringe of outer London. An unusually attractive village, its houses, mostly of mellow red brick and many of the seventeenth and eighteenth centuries, line the single street which leads from the church to the little green and the bridge. To the north of the churchyard is the early-eighteenth-century Charity School, and upstream from the bridge is Denham Place, a characteristic house of the late seventeenth century.

FORDWICH (Kt), once a 'limb' of Sandwich, one of the thriving Cinque Ports, and now a quiet riverside village, was the port for Canterbury when the Stour was navigable (the Caen stone from Normandy for the cathedral was landed here). Beside the river, between the bridge and the charming thirteenth- to fourteenth-century church, is the quaint little Town Hall, a fifteenth-century building whose timber-framing is filled with brick nogging. Among the relics it contains is a ducking-stool for the correction of scolding wives.

HATFIELD BROAD OAK (Ex) is between the roads from Bishops Stortford to Braintree and Harlow to Chelmsford, in rolling country some distance south of Hatfield Forest, one of the few surviving parts of the great forest that covered Essex. The attractive village has some good eighteenth-century brick and gabled timber-framed houses, especially the former Town Farm, of the fifteenth to seventeenth centuries. The large church, mostly of the fourteenth and fifteenth centuries, is the only remaining part of a Benedictine priory founded in 1135.

HAVERING-ATTE-BOWER (Ex), though only a little north of Romford and hence hardly beyond the perimeter of outer London, still manages to retain a genuinely rural air. Set among tall elms round a large green, on which are the old stocks (unusual for Essex), it has some weather-boarded houses. The best of the old buildings, however, is the Bower House, built in 1729 by Henry Flitcroft, a follower of Wren, with brick wings added about 1800.

HURLEY (Bk), between a charming reach of the Thames and the road from Maidenhead to Henley, is an old village with many timber-framed houses. It has also a gabled and timbered sixteenth-century inn, the Old Bell, and a church that belonged to an eleventh-century Benedictine priory, of which there are considerable other medieval remains, including (of the fourteenth century) two large stone barns and a circular dovecot with 600 nesting holes, in a meadow to the west.

MUCH HADHAM (Ht), in the Ash valley between Bishops Stortford and Ware, is an exceptionally delightful village that has been a manor of the Bishops of London since the 11th century. The palace, partly of the fifteenth and sixteenth centuries, is encased in seventeenth-century brick. The village has excellent eighteenth-century houses (The Lordship, Much Hadham Hall, Moor Place) contrasting with humbler sixteenth- and seventeenth-century cottages, some of which have plastered gables with pargetting (see page 98).

TERLING (Ex), in quiet, little-visited country between the roads from Chelmsford to Cambridge and Colchester, is a very attractive village well worth a divergence. Its pleasant houses include the small fifteenth-century timbered manor house north of the church, which itself has an eighteenth-century tower. Terling Place is a large house of about 1780 in white brick, by John Johnson, with curious wings added in 1818.

WARGRAVE (Bk), on the opposite bank of the Thames above Henley, with many riverside houses whose lawns stretch down to the river, is a village much favoured by artists. The signboard of the George and Dragon Inn was painted by two Academicians, C. R. Leslie and Hodgson. The picturesque church, standing beside a backwater, was rebuilt (after being burned down by suffragettes) in 1916, when Norman masonry was revealed beneath the seventeenth-century brick casing of the tower.

WESTMILL (Ht), the most satisfying village in the claylands of Hertfordshire, is just off the main road from Ware to Cambridge. It has many old houses, mainly set about the small green which slopes down to a pleasing row of rough-cast and red-tiled cottages leading towards the church. Above the green is the fine eighteenth-century brick house of Westmill Bury, with a good brick-fronted barn.

WIVENHOE (Ex), on the north bank of the Colne below Colchester and at the beginning of the estuary, is an oyster-breeding and yacht-building village with an attractive quay and many bow windows fronting the water. The church has a tower of about 1500 with a wooden lantern, possibly of the eighteenth century. On the front of the Garrison House in East Street, south of the church, is an intricate pattern of pargetting of about 1650, among the finest work of this kind in the country.

4 East Anglia

No region of England shows a more pronounced individuality in its village building than East Anglia, a term I have used here to include not only Norfolk and Suffolk, but the northern part of Essex as well. Structurally, East Anglia may seem an extension of the chalk country farther south which I have dealt with in Section 2. The geological map shows more than half of this huge promontory as chalkland, and it might be expected that the village features here would resemble those of, say, the Chilterns or the Hertfordshire chalklands. Over the eastern half of East Anglia, however, the chalk is buried under a wide covering of boulder clays, sands and gravels, left by the retreating glaciers towards the end of the great Ice Age. It is these superficial deposits that largely determine the nature of the soil, and it is their occurrence, to some extent at least, that is responsible for the particular characteristics in the villages of this region.

But over and above this, the differences between East Anglia and other regions that are basically chalklands are historical and geographical rather than geological. From the earliest times, this part of

England was cut off from the rest by the impenetrable forests of the
Essex claylands on the south and the equally impassable fenlands
around the Wash on the west. In the second half of the fifth century,
when it began to be settled by the Angles, the region was self-contained within these boundaries and open only to the sea on the north
and east. East Anglia was always one of the most fertile parts of England,
and because of this and the limitations imposed by its natural frontiers,
it became by the time of the Norman Conquest the most populous,
its villages more closely set than those of any other part of the country.

Although the most noticeable geographical difference between
East Anglia and other basic chalklands consists in its being low-lying
country, it is by no means flat. Except for the alluvial stretches round
the lower courses of the rivers and the Broads, most of it can be seen
as gently rolling country, with peaceful, smiling valleys. A large
proportion of the country is given up to arable farming; two-thirds of
the cultivated land in Norfolk, for instance, is under the plough, and
the fields of waving corn are a characteristic feature of the East Anglian
scene in summer.

It was not the corn, however, that was responsible for the prosperity
of East Anglia, but the great industry that laid the foundations of the
nation's wealth towards the end of the Middle Ages. The wool
industry, first developed here with the assistance of Flemish weavers,
who began to come to East Anglia as early as the twelfth century, was
built up through this region's many ports into a thriving trade with
Europe and in particular with the Low Countries. From the fourteenth
century onward, when the cloth began to be woven in England instead of being exported, East Anglia became the most flourishing
region in the country.

Not only was the wool clipped from East Anglian sheep, but it was
brought also from other parts of the country to be made up here. The
industry became centred in two districts: the country around Norwich
and to the north-east of the city, where the village of Worstead gave
its name to a fine woollen yarn; and the country to the west of but
including Ipswich, where Kersey gave its name to the coarse cloth,
woven from long wool, called Kerseymere. The trade continued
unabated until the seventeenth century, though by this time the
Pennine villages were entering into competition. Before the middle of
the nineteenth century, the wool industry of East Anglia was almost

extinct, but its arable farming, neglected during the Middle Ages, had already gained a wide reputation based on the pioneer work done in the eighteenth century by Thomas Coke of Holkham, 'the first farmer in England', and others. Reminders of the great wool period, however, survive in the many beautiful buildings for which East Anglia is famous.

The villages of East Anglia are indeed among the least spoiled and most satisfying in England, and great use is made of the natural materials. Stone in the accepted sense is non-existent, and the very real isolation of this region long prohibited its importation, even for the village church. Because of this, recourse was made to flint from the near-by or underlying chalk, and flintwork has become the distinctive feature of East Anglian building. The most enduring of the local materials, flint has in fact been employed in this region since pre-historic times, and flint-knappers can still be watched at work today at Brandon, on the edge of Breckland.

In many of the simpler (and traditionally older) houses, natural rounded nodules of flint are used, held together with considerable helpings of mortar. Near the north coast, in places where cobbles can easily be collected from the shore, these untrimmed flints are allowed to project in a curious way. Brick is generally used here for the corners, and cottages of this kind are typical of Trimingham, Weybourne and other villages near Cromer. In general, flints whose surface has been worn smooth by water are much to be preferred to those dug up from the ground. In many later and more sophisticated buildings, the flints are dressed, or 'knapped' as it is called, and laid with relatively little mortar, and some very fine craftsmanship is the result.

A speciality of East Anglia, rarely to be met with elsewhere, is the combination of knapped flint and squared freestone that has been developed since the fourteenth century. This chequerwork is seen at its best in Norfolk, where the small flint blocks, usually about four inches square (but sometimes rectangular) and weathered to a darkish grey, give the houses and churches a distinctive regional flavour. More elaborate, and hence usually confined to larger buildings, is the 'flushwork', in which the freestone has a design cut in it and the space thus created is filled with flints, knapped where possible, so that the surface is indeed left flush.

Flintwork is especially to be enjoyed in the patterned walls and tall towers of many East Anglian village churches. Peculiar to this region are the round flint towers, mostly dating apparently from the tenth and eleventh centuries. The round form seems to have been evolved to compensate for the absence of suitable large stones for quoins or corner stones, and these lofty structures may originally have been intended as watch towers. Most of them are near the coast and in the northern half of East Anglia; there are 119 in Norfolk, where they form a striking feature of the landscape, compared with 41 in Suffolk and eight in Essex. The large square towers to be seen everywhere are certainly no less imposing, and many a red-roofed village is dominated by its lofty church tower; that at Winterton, to the north of Yarmouth, for instance, looks out to sea over the sand-dunes which completely hide the village. All this, in combination with the number of thatched roofs, a very exceptional feature, gives the village churches of East Anglia a particular fascination.

In some parts of East Anglia—notably in the Little Ouse valley between Thetford and Diss—the boulder clays have been used to produce 'clay lump'. For this the clay was watered, covered with chopped straw and trodden down by horses; it was then pressed into wooden moulds and left to dry out before being used. Whole villages were built of this material, but as the surface of the walls was almost invariably covered with lime plaster or sometimes (in farm buildings) with tar, it is difficult to distinguish them. On the borders of Cambridgeshire the hardened chalk called 'clunch' was quarried and used for building. Farther north, along the western edge of the chalk, a band of the Lower Greensand has been exposed, and a hard brown stone obtained from this, called carstone ('gingerbread stone' locally), gives a distinctive appearance to the local building between King's Lynn and Hunstanton.

In the southern part of East Anglia, to go to the other extreme, round the borders of Suffolk and Essex, timber was plentiful and it is not surprising that it has found its way into numerous churches and cottages. The timber-framed houses of Suffolk, especially in the great wool district, are certainly not inferior in design and construction to the often more elaborate dwellings of the west Midlands and the Welsh border, and they are, I think, better proportioned and better finished. Lavenham, to take an example, is one of the best-built places in England, the equal, I would like to suggest, of the finest stone-built villages of the Cotswolds.

The infilling of the timber frames was originally of wattle and plaster (occasionally of clay lump), but later the space began to be filled with brick, as this came into favour. The timber, oddly enough, was retained here, as elsewhere, even though it was no longer required structurally. Nothing, it has been said, 'illustrates so well the natural conservatism of the cottage builder; even when his material changed, he saw no reason for altering his style'.

Bricks had been used in East Anglia since the twelfth century (the first were probably imported from the Low Countries, or at least made by immigrant Flemings). By the fifteenth century, they were enjoying a great popularity for the larger and more important buildings, but later they were favoured, too, for the more affluent yeomen farmers' houses. The influence of the Netherlands shows itself clearly in the many houses and farm buildings of the seventeenth century in Suffolk that display curved Flemish gables. Ornamental brickwork in East Anglia, especially of the Tudor period, attains as high a standard as anywhere. As the timber began to be thinned out, more and more bricks found their way into cottage walls, particularly at a distance from the flint areas. Bricks and pantiles made from the local clays are responsible for the bright colours of the buildings in many villages.

Pantiles (tiles curved transversely to an ogee shape) were first introduced from Holland in the seventeenth century, but were not made in this country until the following century. They were used extensively in East Anglia, however, during the next 150 years or so. But the natural roofing material is thatch, made from corn straw or (better) of reeds from the broads and marshes of Norfolk. There are more thatched roofs in East Anglia than in any other part of England, and the thatch here is perhaps the neatest and firmest of any, if less picturesque than that of Devon and Somerset.

Common everywhere in East Anglia is the plain white plastered wall beneath a thatched roof. This plastering was first adopted on the fronts of brick buildings to preserve them from the weather, but it was later employed also to conceal the structure of timber-framed houses when these were no longer the fashion. Through a curious change in taste, the reverse process has set in and it is now *de rigueur* to strip off the plaster and reveal the timbers.

A speciality of the southern part of East Anglia is the working of ornamental patterns, sometimes of great elaboration, in the plaster, an art known as 'pargetting'. This attained its richest development in the seventeenth century, though in fact it was introduced more than a hundred years before (a guild of pargetters was established in London as early as 1501). The designs, usually worked in relief, were at first merely geometrical patterns, but later swags and scrolls and elaborate arrangements of flowers and foliage made their appearance. The most ornate work is naturally in the towns, such as Ipswich and Saffron Walden, but pargetting is to be seen also in many of the larger villages and it has extended as well to the neighbouring regions and occasionally farther afield.

Villages of East Anglia

BOXFORD (Sf) is on a tributary of the Stour and the road from Sudbury to Ipswich. The old church, in the centre of this large and pleasant village, has a remarkable fourteenth-century porch built of timber. There are picturesque timber-framed cottages facing the church, and other good houses, farther north, include Old Chequers, with a carved bressumer, Hendrick House, which has an eighteenth-century plastered front, and Old Castle House, where the early nineteenth-century front is stuccoed.

CASTLE ACRE (Nf), to the north of Swaffham and west of the Fakenham road, stands on the old Roman road of the Peddar's Way. Most of the village is built with material from the large Cluniac priory, the picturesque ruins of which remain (particularly the beautiful late-Norman west front and the late-fifteenth-century gatehouse), or from the Norman castle, the thirteenth-century Barbican of which spans the village street. The church, mainly of the thirteenth and fifteenth centuries, is between the priory and the castle.

CASTLE RISING (Nf), on the road from King's Lynn to Hunstanton, is perhaps the most interesting village in Norfolk, with houses built of 'carstone' from the greensand formations. It has also the ruins of a massive Norman castle of about 1150, enclosed by earthworks; a delightful if rather over-restored Norman church of the twelfth century; and the early-seventeenth-century Trinity Hospital, a bedehouse founded as a charity for ten elderly women.

CAVENDISH (Sf) is in the Stour valley between Clare and Sudbury. The centre of the village is a large green which slopes up northward to an attractive group of thatched cottages. Above these rises the tall

18 *Lavenham, Suffolk*

early-fourteenth-century tower of the church, its stair-turret surmounted by a triangular wooden bellcote. There are several sixteenth-century houses in the village, among them the Old Rectory, near the pond, and the farmhouse of Nether Hall, north of the church.

CLAVERING (Ex), a few miles west of Newport, on the little Stort, is an exceptionally attractive and secluded village most of the houses of which are on an island between two roads. In the road leading to the fine church, built of pebble rubble in the fifteenth century, are two especially interesting houses: one of the fifteenth century with a long overhanging upper storey and the other of the seventeenth century with an unusual shop front.

DEDHAM (Ex), on the Stour east of the Colchester–Ipswich road, was engaged in the flourishing wool trade in the fourteenth to seventeenth centuries, and is one of the most handsome villages in East Anglia. It consists chiefly of a single street with notable timber-framed buildings, including the Sun Hotel, of the early sixteenth century, and others in eighteenth-century white and red brick, among them the grammar school and the elaborately-decorated Shermans. With its side to the street is the long and dignified church of the late fifteenth century whose tower of knapped flint was a favourite subject with Constable.

EAST BERGHOLT (Sf), north-east of Dedham and on the other side of the Stour, was the birthplace in 1776 of John Constable, who has immortalised the surrounding country in his landscapes. The village can show many good timber-framed and plastered houses of the sixteenth century and later. The picturesque fifteenth- to sixteenth-century church has an unfinished tower at the west end; it was deprived of its steeple, says local legend, by the devil, and the bells are hung in a curious wooden cage of about 1500 in the churchyard.

FINCHINGFIELD (Ex), which lies in fertile country some distance south-west of the road from Colchester to Cambridge, is one of the most beautiful villages in England. From the church, built of pebble rubble in the fourteenth century, except for the Norman tower, the road winds down to the brick bridge and the pond, with the large green beyond. The village has a delightful variety of old houses showing plastered timber-work (as in the old

19 *Finchingfield, Essex*

guildhall of about 1500 beside the church), eighteenth-century brick and much red tiling.

GREAT BARDFIELD (Ex), on the river Pant, a tributary of the Blackwater, a little south of Finchingfield, is a village of quiet charm. Its most attractive houses, including timber-framed cottages, mostly with plastered fronts, the sixteenth-century Place House (timber with a brick infilling) and a fine eighteenth-century house with brick chequerwork, all lie along the road leading to the fourteenth-century church, near which is the timber-framed and plastered Hall, built about 1600.

HORNING (Nf), north-east of Norwich and north-west of Great Yarmouth, is a pretty village on the Broads, that region of level meadowlands traversed by meandering waterways which seem to merge imperceptibly into wide, shallow lakes. It has gained much favour as a boating and yachting centre and is liable to be too popular in summer. It really consists of two villages, Upper Street and Lower Street, but the latter has become a residential centre.

HOXNE (Sf), in the Waveney valley south of the Diss–Bungay road, is approached by a little brick bridge over the river. The centre of the village is a small triangular green with tall limes, and from this the main street ascends to the church, which has a splendid fifteenth-century tower. Hoxne has a variety of attractive old houses—brick, plaster-fronted or timber-framed, with roofs of thatch, tile or slate—peeping out between the trees.

KERSEY (Sf), which lies north-west of Hadleigh and the Ipswich–Sudbury road, owes its very lovely appearance to the cloth-making industry. The situation of the village is unusual in that its one long street lies across instead of along the little river Brett. There are many charming houses, some of brick and some timber-framed and mostly plastered over, some with overhanging fronts, lining the steep hills on either side of the picturesque ford. River House has a mid-sixteenth-century porch and Woodbine Cottage is claimed to be of pre-Reformation origin. The church, with its tall grey fifteenth-century tower, stands aloof on the hill at the south end of the village.

LAVENHAM (Sf), some distance east of the road from Sudbury to Bury St Edmunds, is the most handsome and prosperous-looking village in East Anglia (though almost large enough to be called a town). It has a spacious and beautiful church, built between 1484 and 1530, and a wealth of lovely timber-framed houses. Among the few that can be mentioned are the impressive early-sixteenth-century Guildhall dominating the Market Place, the charming late-fourteenth-century gabled and timbered Swan Hotel in the High Street, the Old Wool Hall and the former Grammar School, both of the fifteenth century, in Water Street, and others here and in Church Street and Shilling Street.

LONG MELFORD (Sf), like Lavenham, is almost a town, and like Lavenham and Sudbury, was an important centre of the wool industry in the fourteenth to sixteenth centuries. It has one of the most magnificent parish churches in England, built of freestone in the late fifteenth century and showing a lavish display of flush-work. The church stands at the upper end of the green, delightful with its lofty elms, and on either side lower down are two fine ranges of building: Melford Hall, an imposing turreted mansion built in 1552, and Trinity Hospital, Elizabethan, but much restored. In the immensely long main street are many timber-framed houses—among them the interesting Bull Hotel, dating from about 1450—and others of eighteenth-century brick.

NEWPORT (Ex), on the road from Bishops Stortford to Cambridge, is a village of unusual distinction, with a fine large church, mainly of the thirteenth to fifteenth centuries, and many notable sixteenth- and seventeenth-century houses in its long street, some enriched with pargetting, the best in any village in England. Particularly admirable is the Crown Inn, built about 1600 and given its pargetted decoration in 1692. Among other pleasant houses by the green is Martin's Farm, which has a timbered fifteenth-century front.

ORFORD (Sf), once a port of considerable importance at the mouth of the Ore, is now a delightful old-world village on the Alde, which has cut off the Ore and runs parallel to the sea for nearly 10 miles, separated from it only by a narrow spit of shingle. Orford has a massive 18-sided keep built in 1167 for Henry II, a fourteenth-century church with a ruined late-Norman chancel attached, and many pleasing brick-and-timber houses and others in which fossils from the Coral Crag of which they are built can be seen.

STOKE-BY-NAYLAND (Sf), whose handsome fifteenth-century church tower, 120 feet high, was another favoured subject with Constable, lies in the meadows between the Stour and the Box, east of the Sudbury–Colchester road. It has two good early-seventeenth-century timber-framed houses, the Guildhall and the Maltings, west of the church in Back Street, and a great many neat timber-framed and plastered cottages.

WOOLPIT (Sf), on the road between Bury St Edmunds and Stowmarket, has a fourteenth- to fifteenth-century church with a variety of flushwork and a conspicuous spire raised in 1845, and a village street with seventeenth- and eighteenth-century houses, some timber-framed, some of red brick. Among these latter is the Swan Inn, which is of two periods, the two lower storeys of the eighteenth century, the upmost of the early nineteenth century. White bricks from Woolpit have been used, among other places, in the Senate wing of the Capitol in Washington, completed in 1827.

5 The Fens and Lincolnshire

In this section I have covered the whole of Lincolnshire, including the chalk and limestone country, and also the region round The Wash known as the Fens, or Fenland. This is the most extensive tract of very low land in England, and it possesses a strong and indeed unique individuality.

The Fens were originally an enormously wide but shallow bay created by the combined estuaries of the Witham, the Welland, the Nene and the Great Ouse. (Alternatively, this can be thought of as a huge sunken valley made when these rivers cut a great gap through the chalklands that stood as a barrier along the east coast.) The Fens, which extend over 60 miles from north to south and some 40 miles from east to west, were formed by the gradual silting up of the bay, and all that now survives of this is The Wash. The immense expanse of flat land hardly anywhere rises to as much as 50 feet above the sea and it stretches for mile after mile unrelieved by anything more than the merest swelling.

When the Anglo-Saxon invaders arrived, they found the Fens an impenetrable swamp, though later its few 'islands' provided an ade-

quate refuge against the Vikings, until these new invaders discovered how to navigate the sluggish reed-fringed rivers. Most of the few hillocks that raise themselves above the marsh are made noticeable by the towns and villages built on them—Ely cathedral and Boston 'stump' are well-known landmarks—but important settlements, like Peterborough and Cambridge, grew up also along the margins of the Fens.

Of this vast swamp, practically nothing survives today, except for a few areas, like Wicken Fen, that have been specially preserved. The first attempts to drain the Fens are believed to have been made by the Romans, but the drainage was not undertaken on a serious scale until the seventeenth century and the work was not in fact completed until the beginning of the nineteenth century. Until their reclamation, the Fens were not only the most inaccessible lands in England, they were the poorest, but the ground won from the marsh proved extremely fertile and this has naturally led to very intensive farming, so that the Fens now support a larger population than many more congenial areas.

The pattern of settlement in the Fens, as might be expected, is noticeably different from that of the rest of the country. There are very few ancient villages; most of them date from after the beginning of the great reclamation. The subsoil of the Fens is actually of two kinds: a belt of silt washed up by the sea and forming a low ridge some two to four miles inland, stretching from Wainfleet via Boston to Spalding and thence to King's Lynn; and a bed of peat from soil brought down by the rivers, spreading inland behind the silt ridge. The first settlements were nucleated villages, all lying along the ridge of silt. But even in Saxon times, settlers had begun to penetrate into the inhospitable marshes and make themselves new farmsteads and hamlets. From the parent villages on the ridge, winding roads were pushed out, where the marshlands permitted, to the solitary settlements on either side which can be seen as successive frontiers established in the battle against the marshes and the sea. The villages in consequence are small and scattered irregularly over the landscape. The marshes did not lend themselves to the common Saxon form of open-field agriculture. As Dr Hoskins has pointed out, the map of an open-field parish, at least before the enclosures of the eighteenth century, shows the original settlement with empty fields surrounding it and com-

21 *Folkingham, Lincolnshire*

paratively few hamlets and farmsteads. The map of the Fens, on the other hand, is speckled with the names of hamlets and farms, all strung together by an intricate network of lanes.

To the south-east of the Fens, on the border of East Anglia, stretches the wide expanse of flat, desolate land known as Breckland. This was always intractable and unrewarding country (the record of 'deserted villages' is evidence of this) and very sparsely populated. The villages are mostly to be found along the few rivers, and for mile after mile one sees no dwellings at all. This sense of desolation is enhanced by the solid ranks of pines in the dull plantations that now cover much of the country. Good building material was always difficult to come by, and even in prehistoric times pits had to be dug in the sandy subsoil to get at the flints in the chalk below. (Flint knapping still thrives at Brandon, as I mentioned in the previous section.) Here, as in the Fens, the villagers had to put up with inferior timber (poplar and lime, for instance) for the framework of their houses, and even these woods became so scarce that a royal proclamation in 1604 charged the people to make their houses of brick or stone, and the cutting of timber, even for firewood, had to stop.

The deposits which make up the Fenland push also along the coast of Lincolnshire and are extended across the Plain of Holderness beyond the Humber. Geologically, Lincolnshire is divided into four strips stretching north and south: a belt of lias on the west belonging to the Midland Plain (which we shall meet later), a strip of limestone that is the county's most familiar feature, a wide belt of chalk that includes the Lincolnshire Wolds, and the strip of coastal deposits just mentioned. If we were considering geology alone, we would put the limestone in Section 7 and the chalk in Section 2, but in fact these outcrops are disappointing in that they show few of the characteristics which are so pronounced farther south, and (if I may labour this point) the villages have much more in common with others in the county than with those of similar geological regions.

The most noticeable feature in the notoriously flat country, as I say, is the long ridge of limestone known as The Cliff, running due north and south, with a steep if not high escarpment on the west, a barrier broken only at Lincoln, where it is penetrated by the Witham. What it lacks in height it makes up for by its straightness and the fact that it looks out over a great expanse of level country. The Cliff has a long dip slope on the east, mostly unrelieved by trees or valleys, reaching down to a broad clay trough between it and the Wolds. This gently sloping plateau remained practically uncultivated until the call for more corn during the Napoleonic wars brought it under the plough. As a result, there are few villages of any age and even these are mostly poor and unattractive. Along the western face of The Cliff, on the other hand, there are many small settlements, spaced with almost monotonous regularity along the spring line.

The Lincolnshire Wolds, a region of quietly undulating chalkland, reach a very moderate height and show no marked escarpment. In the northern part there are large farms but few villages; such villages as exist are mostly small and confined to the dry streamless valleys. But in the southern part the chalk is covered with tracts of boulder clay and other deposits similar to those we found in East Anglia, and here settlements are spread rather thicker. The term 'wold', incidentally, has the same derivation as Weald, so these uplands, now rather bare, must once have been covered by woods.

Despite the existence of chalk and limestone in the county, by far the commonest material for village building is brick. The oldest brick building in Lincolnshire is the large gatehouse of Thornton Abbey, dating from 1382; the most famous is Tattershall Castle, completed by 1440. In the fifteenth century brick was being used on a wide scale for the larger buildings and from the seventeenth century, when timber— at least the better timber, like oak—was becoming scarce, village building almost everywhere was in brick. Chalk stone was dug from the Wolds near Louth to some extent, but there seem to be no flint buildings in this region. Sandstone was also quarried from the fringe of greensand round the southern part of the Wolds from the fifteenth century, and is to be seen in churches here and there, but for house building it was rejected in favour of the more popular brick.

Though thatch is a familiar sight in Lincolnshire and the Fens (where sedge is still cut occasionally for new roofing), tiles are much more in evidence. Pantiles, introduced into this region (as in East Anglia) in the seventeenth century, were in general use by the end of the eighteenth; they are more common than plain tiles on the older buildings, except in south-west Lincolnshire, where Colly Weston stone slates from over the border in Northamptonshire have always been in much demand. But the ordinary, unpretentious dwellings of this region of England are built of plain brick and pantile, relieved by some plaster with its attendant thatch in the more prosperous villages.

The architectural pride of all this country, however, lies not in picturesque or well-built villages, but in its strong ecclesiastical tradition. Many of the fine Lincolnshire churches are built of the oolitic limestone from Ancaster, between Grantham and Sleaford, and in the Fens considerable use is made of oolitic stone from quarries near Stamford. The difficulty of transporting stone, except by water, meant that it was reserved almost wholly for churches, though even in the villages of the limestone belt in Lincolnshire little use is made of freestone. The older cottages here, dating mostly from the seventeenth and eighteenth centuries, are built almost entirely of rubble masonry (*i.e.* rough, irregular fragments of stone).

Villages of the Fens and Lincolnshire

BOLINGBROKE (Li) is at the southern end of the Wolds, between the roads from Spilsby to Horncastle and Sleaford. Pleasantly situated, it is also one of the more attractive of the characteristically simple red-brick villages of this part of Lincolnshire, and has fine fourteenth-century windows in its church. Of the twelfth-century castle there survive considerable earthworks and a little of the masonry; it passed in the fourteenth century to John of Gaunt, whose son, Henry IV, was born here.

CHIPPENHAM (Ca), west of the road between Mildenhall and Newmarket, has more character than any village lying on the edge of the Fens. It consists almost wholly of the thirteenth- to fifteenth-century church (built of flint and pebble rubble, with a fifteenth-century tower), an early-eighteenth-century school in brick, and two streets of model cottages of about 1800. These end abruptly with a prospect of dead flat fields reminiscent more of Holland than England.

FEN DRAYTON (Ca) is between the river Ouse and the road from Cambridge to Huntingdon. To the north-east of the church, which was built of pebble rubble in the fourteenth century, is a thatched cottage popularly associated with Cornelius Vermuyden, the Dutch engineer who was responsible for draining much of the Fens in the first half of the seventeenth century. The stone doorway, however, though inscribed 'Niet zonder Arbyt', is dated 1713. The Three Tuns Inn has a timber-framed gable and there are other interesting houses in the village.

FOLKINGHAM (Li), on the road from Lincoln to Peterborough and about halfway between the two, was once a coaching town of some importance. It still has many eighteenth-century houses and inns round its central open space, which, oddly enough, is not an original market place but was created by pulling down the town hall and other buildings. At one end is the fine large twelfth- to fifteenth-century church; at the other a stone manor house of about 1670.

FULBECK (Li), on the main road between Grantham and Lincoln, which follows the limestone escarpment of The Cliff, may claim with some justification to be the prettiest village in Lincolnshire, though it lacks the richness and character of the limestone villages farther south. The main street, which has cottages of the local warm-hued stone, roofed with glowing pantiles, slopes pleasantly up from the plain to the church, set on the hill of a small green.

GREATFORD (Li) is another stone-built village, though off the limestone and in the valley of the Glen north of the Stamford–Spalding road. The village is set among trees, and a stone bridge crosses the little river, which here spreads out into a pleasant tree-shaded pool, with trim green margins. The road from the bridge, lined with lime trees, leads up towards the church, which has a graceful thirteenth-century broach spire of Ancaster stone.

HEMINGFORD GREY (Hu), on the banks of the smoothly gliding Ouse between Godmanchester and St Ives, is a village of exquisite loveliness with many charming sixteenth- and seventeenth-century black-and-white timber-framed houses, as well as red-brick houses of the late seventeenth and eighteenth centuries, near the river, where the fifteenth-century church looks out over the lush green meadows. The manor house is one of the finest examples of medieval domestic architecture in the country.

LEIGHTON BROMSWOLD (Hu), on rising ground between two tributaries of the Ouse, north of the Huntingdon–Kettering road, has a grass-bordered main street lined with delightful seventeenth-century cottages, and a fine church that is a mixture of Gothic and classical styles. This was built for George Herbert, the poet, who was incumbent here in 1626–30. The vicarage was converted out of an early-seventeenth-century gatehouse intended to be the entrance to a castle that in fact was never built.

SOMERSBY (Li), in a quiet valley of the Wolds several miles east of Horncastle, is a charming little village with a small fifteenth-century church containing memorials of Lord Tennyson, who was born in 1809 in the picturesque cream-washed house close by, at that time the rectory. In the churchyard is a fine fifteenth-century cross, and behind there is a pleasant view of the rolling country of the Wolds.

THORNEY (Ca), on the road from Peterborough to Wisbech, in the middle of the vast Bedford Level, has a church which retains most of the early-twelfth-century nave built as part of a Benedictine monastery. The eighteenth-century houses round the pleasant green, including the vicarage, incorporate other remains of the abbey, and on the west, behind high walls, is Thorney Abbey House, partly of the sixteenth century, partly of 1660. The village also contains model buildings of the mid-nineteenth century.

6 Between the Chalk and the Limestone

If we wished to reduce the geological structure of England to the simplest pattern, we should divide the country into four sections: (1) the Weald and Greensand region, with the North and South Downs; (2) the South-West, comprising Devon and Cornwall and part of Somerset; (3) the six northern counties, that is, the country roughly north of a line from the Mersey to the Humber; and (4) the rest, which in fact is larger than all the other sections put together. I make this distinction because I want for a moment to consider this major part of England as a whole.

It is well known that if you take a journey across England from south-west to north-east, say from Hampshire to Norfolk or from Dorset to Lincolnshire, you are likely to travel all the time on one geological outcrop; in these instances, the chalk or the limestone. But if you leave London and go north-westward in the direction of Liverpool, you will cross all the various outcrops in turn. It follows that if you travel from south-west to north-east, you can expect to come across the same kind of building stones and see villages of the same style and character, but if you go from London to Liverpool you will notice a variety of building materials and in consequence a similar diversity in the villages.

The reason for this, if I may reduce it to simple terms, is that the different geological deposits, after being laid down on a level bed (mostly in a great shallow lake), were then tipped up, rather as in the Wealden country, only here they were all pushed up from the north-west corner. As a result the strata all dip down towards the south-east, but as the softer materials were worn away, the harder rocks like the chalk and limestone were left as long outcrops running from south-west to north-east. Because of this we have between the chalk and the limestone a long wide valley, composed of sands and clays, running in the same direction as the outcrops.

The geological map of Britain will make this pattern clear, but as it deals with the fundamental structure and is not concerned with what happens on the surface, it ignores the clay and shows only a narrow band of the greensands between the chalk and the limestone. But all along its length, the limestone, as it dips to the south-east, does in fact pass underneath a belt of clay which fills the wide valley extending to the greensands which border the chalklands. This clay belt stretches from Frome in Somerset through Chippenham, Oxford and Bedford until it reaches the Fens; it can be traced by the upper courses of the Bristol Avon and the Thames and the whole course of the Great Ouse. These perhaps originally formed one great river flowing out into The Wash, but the Avon now flows in the other direction, forcing its way through the limestone, while the Thames, after leaving a valley north of the Vale of White Horse, turns east of the vale and penetrates the chalk escarpment between the Berkshire Downs and the Chilterns.

The line where the limestone dips below the clay belt is marked by a succession of towns and villages which prospered because of the advantages to be gained from both regions. Not only did they benefit from the better water supply where the springs came out at the edge of the limestone, but a much more varied agriculture could be practised in their neighbourhood, making use of the light dry soils of the limestone on the one side and the comparatively heavy soils of the clay on the other. On the clay, great areas are taken up by meadowland, the basis of the very profitable cattle rearing and dairy farming.

These claylands do not form just a simple basin, however. They are divided along part of their length by an outcrop of grey-blue Corallian limestone, of very moderate elevation, but showing as a line of quite distinctive hills in this broad level vale. Oxford in fact owes its position to the gap which the Thames has created in this discontinuous ridge. The stone obtained from the outcrop, usually called Coral Rag (it consists chiefly of corals and other fossilised shells), has been used extensively in the villages between the Vale of White Horse and the upper Thames, but it is a rugged lumpish stone and, like undressed flint, needs a great deal of mortar.

A band of the Lower Greensand, similar to that we saw in the Weald, runs parallel to the chalk escarpment from Leighton Buzzard until it reaches the Fens; it is most prominent in the heights round Woburn Sands. The stone from this outcrop, too, has been used for local building, and in some churches the yellow-brown sandstone has been combined quite effectively with the chalk from the neighbouring downs. But the standard material for building in this predominantly clay country, as in the other clay regions, is brick.

Bricks have been made extensively in this region since the early fifteenth century, and brickwork of the best is to be seen in such a village as Ewelme. Building in brick had become quite general by the end of the sixteenth century, and it was given a big push forward here, as elsewhere in the south, by the demand for bricks after the Great Fire of London. But the great boom came with the production, from 1880 onwards, of cheap bricks from the miscalled Oxford Clay around Bedford and Peterborough. Soon machine-made bricks were not only being used in these districts, but were being sent by rail all over the country and especially to the new industrial villages of the north midlands and the north. The gaunt forests of tall chimneys and the harsh landscape of huge clay-pits are the visible and ugly sign of this flourishing industry.

The covering of brickwork (and other surfaces) with roughcast—a mixture of coarse sand and gravel or stone chippings with lime and (nowadays) cement—though of course met with all over England, is particularly common in the villages of this region. The roof covering is normally tile for the older buildings, slate for the newer; but some

22 *Ewelme, Oxfordshire*

fine examples of straw thatching are still to be seen. Stone from the great limestone belt has been used in Oxford for the colleges, and here and in other towns for many of the public buildings, but it has been reserved in most of the villages of the claylands for the church and sometimes the manor house. Nevertheless, the villages of this region are among the most varied and charming in England. As we approach the limestone, for instance, we pass from villages which are mainly of brick, with an occasional timber-framed building, to others where brick, timber-framed and stone houses can be seen side by side, before reaching those famous Cotswold villages that are built completely of stone.

Villages between the Chalk and the Limestone

ASHTON KEYNES (Wt), which lies some distance south-west of the road from Swindon to Cirencester, is one of the first villages to be passed by the stripling Thames and one of the most enchanting. The village is actually built round a large rectangle of roads, and the river circumnavigates it, passing under a succession of bridges, with the cottages, of stone from the not-too-distant Cotswolds, set back behind margins of green. The Transitional Norman church, beyond the river, is approached through a long avenue of elms.

BRILL (Bu) stands aloof on an isolated hill of the Corallian limestone which is avoided by the road from Thame to Bicester. The large village is built almost entirely of brick round a green and a square. To the south of the square is the sixteenth-century manor house, and from the north side streets lead up to a seventeenth-century post-mill on the top of the hill, which affords a wonderful view over the vale in every direction, but especially towards the escarpment of the Chilterns.

BUSCOT (Bk), which spans the Lechlade–Faringdon road, is a pleasant little village, mostly laid out in 1897, with stone cottages, in the peaceful country of the upper Thames. The Adam-style manor house of 1780 (later altered), to the south-east in a fine park, and the seventeenth-century rectory, together with the farmlands and woods running down to the willow-fringed river, all now happily belong to the National Trust.

CASTLE EATON (Wt) is on the south bank of the Thames between the roads from Swindon to Cirencester and Lechlade, and at some

23 *Hartest, Suffolk*
24 *Steeple Morden, Cambridgeshire*

considerable distance from both. Approached by devious lanes through the level meadows, it is a surprising and delightful village, mostly of stone from the Cotswolds, though the Red Lion Inn, beside the small green, is of charming brickwork. The church, partly Norman and partly thirteenth century, has an unusual stone turret for the sanctus bell.

COLESHILL (Bk), climbing the slope of the Corallian limestone ridge above the river Cole, between Faringdon and Highworth, is a village with model cottages of about 1870 built of the local stone but faced and roofed with Cotswold limestone. Overlooked by the fifteenth-century tower of its church, it stands outside the park of Coleshill House, a seventeenth-century mansion usually attributed to Inigo Jones but more likely by Sir Roger Pratt. The village, with Badbury Hill to the east, affording views over the upper Thames and the Vale of White Horse, now belongs to the National Trust.

CUXHAM (Ox), a little west of Watlington, below the face of the Chiltern escarpment, is a quiet village set among trees with a little stream running through it. The cottages show a mingling of stone and grey and red brick, with (rather unusually) some weather-boarding, and thatched and tiled roofs. The small church, which has a Norman west doorway, lies off the road, among farm buildings, peering over the roofs of a row of thatched cottages.

DORCHESTER (Ox), where the busy road from Henley to Oxford crosses the river Thame near its junction with the Thames, was a Roman settlement and an important Saxon town, for some time the cathedral city of Wessex, and its splendid abbey church shows work of many periods from the twelfth to the seventeenth century. The very attractive village street, too, has a variety of charming old houses, mostly of brick, with tiled roofs, but with some timberwork here and there.

ELSTOW (Bd), on the Luton road just south of Bedford, is inseparably connected with the name of John Bunyan. Though now almost a suburb, it still manages to retain much of the atmosphere of a rural village. On the exceptionally ample green, where Bunyan saw his first 'vision', stands the sixteenth-century Moot Hall, its narrow-spaced timbers filled with brick nogging; it now contains a museum of seventeenth-century rural life. At the edge of the green is the over-restored church, partly Norman, with a detached fifteenth-century tower in which Bunyan rang the bells in his youth.

EWELME (Ox), almost a Chiltern village (except that it is built in brick), lies in a fold below the escarpment, north of the Henley–Oxford road. One of the most delightful villages in England, it has pleasant cottages of fine brickwork with flowery gardens; but its chief distinction is in the handsome church at the upper end, built of flint and stone with brick parapets, and the adjoining brick-built almshouses and school, all of which were founded in the mid-fifteenth century by William de la Pole, a minister of Henry VI.

LONG CRENDON (Bu), just north of Thame on the road to Bicester, is a scattered village with many brick and timbered houses of the fifteenth to seventeenth centuries, some thatched with straw, and one eighteenth-century house of chequered brick that has a carriageway adjoining under a thatched roof. Close to the churchyard is the long fourteenth-century Courthouse or staple hall, partly timber-framed, and probably used originally as a wool store. Long Crendon Manor, south of the village, is a fifteenth- to sixteenth-century house approached through a gatehouse mainly of the fifteenth century.

OLD WARDEN (Bd), in pleasantly wooded country enclosed by the triangle of roads connecting Bedford, Biggleswade and Shefford, is a delightfully kept village with a range of Victorian model cottages of neat design, an early piece of country planning. They were built by the first Lord Ongley (who died in 1877) outside the gates of his park. The fine church, mostly of the thirteenth to fifteenth centuries, is rich in sixteenth- and seventeenth-century Continental wood carving brought here by Lord Ongley.

SHRIVENHAM (Bk), in the Vale of White Horse on the road from Swindon to Faringdon, is a large village some of whose houses of warm-coloured limestone, with stone or thatched roofs, stand behind an avenue of limes through which the main road passes. The seventeenth-century late-Gothic church retains its previous, fifteenth-century, tower. The establishment here in 1946 of the Military College of Science has led to a considerable extension of the village, with a consequent loss to its character.

SUTTON COURTENAY (Bk) is an exceptionally charming village on a quiet backwater of the Thames, reached from the Abingdon–Newbury road. The interesting thirteenth- to fifteenth-century church stands at the edge of the spacious green, which is shaded by some fine trees, and there is a variety of houses of the sixteenth to eighteenth centuries. The house called Norman Hall, opposite the church, dates partly from about 1200, and that to the south, named The Abbey, incorporates remains of a Benedictine grange. At the west end of the village is the gabled sixteenth-century manor house of the Courtenays.

WESTON UNDERWOOD (Bu) is a delightful village to the west of Olney, on the edge of the limestone country. The road, passing some fine stables and barns, leads through gate-piers into what was once the great park of Weston House, a mansion pulled down early in the last century. The village street has many fine fifteenth-century houses, but its focus is the long front of the late-seventeenth-century house once occupied by the poet William Cowper.

7 The Limestone Country

The great limestone belt which can be called the architectural backbone of England runs diagonally across country from south-west to north-east, extending from Portland Bill on the Dorset coast through the Cotswold Hills, Edgehill, the Northamptonshire uplands and the Lincoln Cliff to the Humber. It reappears in the moorlands of North Yorkshire, where it culminates in the Cleveland Hills and the great line of cliffs between Filey and Saltburn.

The limestone country can be divided conveniently into five sections: the outcrops south of the Bristol Avon in Somerset and Dorset, with a detached outlier in the Isle of Purbeck; the Cotswolds, where the villages are at their finest; the country north-east of the Cotswolds, rather less determinate but extending to Northamptonshire and Rutland; the Lincoln Cliff and its hinterland (included in Section 5); and finally, the North Yorkshire Moors, which I have reserved for the section on the country east of the Pennines.

For the most part, the limestone forms a long series of ridges and escarpments, not unlike the chalk in this respect (it was moulded to the same pattern, as I explained in the previous section), but it

25 *Lacock, Wiltshire*

reaches a higher elevation than the chalk and it differs considerably in other ways, the most important of which is that it provides a perfect building stone. The term 'limestone belt', as has been pointed out before, is an over-simplification if it leads one to believe that we have here to deal with one consistent, unvarying stone. In fact, the stone varies noticeably from one district to another and even quarries in the same district may yield different textures and qualities of stone. In North Yorkshire the limestone differs so greatly from that south of the Humber that it almost seems another kind of stone.

The main limestone belt is actually made up of two layers of stone; oolitic and liassic. The oolite, which (to speak again in simple terms) is the upper stratum, is a lovely stone varying in colour from silver-grey to pale yellow and composed largely of tiny granules or beads of calcium carbonate, pressed tightly together so that they rather resemble the fish's roe from which the stone gets its name. The oolite is convenient to quarry, as most of the beds lie at or near the surface, and it is comparatively soft and easy to work when first cut. It mellows under exposure to the air, and this as much as anything else has contributed to the beauty of the Cotswold and Northamptonshire villages.

The lias, on the other hand—the lower stratum—is an inferior building stone that often weathers poorly. There are really two kinds of lias in England, the Lower and the Middle, and they are quite different from each other in their composition. The Lower Lias we shall see on the Midland Plain; it is the Middle bed that concerns us here. A hard calcareous marlstone, mostly light brown in colour, it appears only where the over-lying oolite has been eroded or where the limestone escarpment has been weathered back to leave outlying hills or ridges. Bredon Hill in Worcestershire, for example, is made up of the Middle Lias with a harder cap of oolite.

The finest section of the limestone belt, both scenically and, as I say, for its villages, is the Cotswolds, stretching from the lovely old city of Bath, on the Bristol Avon, nearly as far as Stratford, on the Warwickshire Avon, a distance of almost 60 miles. In this section, the land rises gradually from the vales of the Upper Thames and its northern tributaries to a high plateau, from the edge of which it falls away steeply in an escarpment facing north-west over the Vale of Severn and the Midland Plain. Though the villages here do not shun the bare

26 *Ashby St Ledgers, Northamptonshire*
27 *Ketton, Rutland*

hilltops, as they tend to do on the chalk, there are few of any size on the higher parts of the uplands; most of them are tucked away in sheltered places in the valleys, hemmed in by steep hills—like Castle Combe, one of the most famous, on the stream which joins the Avon above Bath. There is, however, a greater diversity of village sites in the Cotswolds than almost anywhere else (except perhaps in Devon): villages will be found not only beside the streams in valley bottoms, but running up or along the sides of hills at precipitous angles. In some of the deeper glens, such as those made by the Bristol Avon and the Gloucestershire Frome (the Golden Valley), the villages are engagingly built along the tree-covered slopes.

A great many of the Cotswold villages, like those of the best building districts of East Anglia, began to be rebuilt during the Tudor period, by which time they had become thriving centres of the great wool industry. The trade in fact flourished right through from the later Middle Ages to the eighteenth century, but the finest period for domestic building lasted from about 1580 to 1690, and the characteristic Cotswold village dates from this time, when, too, many of the manor houses were rebuilt by the prosperous wool merchants. The wide main streets of numerous Cotswold villages, designed to serve as market places, are evidence of the significance of the wool trade. Though the importance of these villages declined when wool was no longer required on so large a scale and when the northern villages entered into competition, many of their houses and other buildings have survived untouched since the sixteenth and seventeenth centuries. Three centuries of prosperity based on wool, combined with the existence of the finest and most natural building material, have made the Cotswolds the outstanding architectural region of England.

The rural craftsmen who built the villages of the Cotswolds (and to a hardly less extent those of Northamptonshire) took full advantage of their supreme material. Three things contribute to the harmony of the Cotswold village: the beautiful weathering properties of the oolitic limestone, the remarkably high quality of the mason's work, and the fact that all the buildings in the village, from the church to the humblest cottage, are of the same noble stone. From floor to roof-top, and from one village to the next, the same satisfying material was used. The stone for the church and other important buildings might be brought some distance from a well-known quarry, while that for the average house was always obtained locally. But throughout the whole region we sense a basic unity and a simplicity combined with dignity of thought and expression. Unlike other regions, moreover, we have no need to search here for examples of the best period among later building: whole villages in this style still dominate the countryside. It has been well said of the Cotswold villages that 'there is no other district in England that has expressed so simply and so beautifully in terms of building, the unity between the soil, the dwelling and its inhabitants'. In no other part of the country, not even East Anglia, does the village seem to fit so naturally into the landscape.

Mr Alec Clifton-Taylor, in his scholarly study, *The Pattern of English Building*, speaks of 'the many and beautiful refinements which are associated with the Cotswold style of building. The late retention of well-moulded mullioned windows; the elaborate labels or drip-stones, dropped down a few inches at each end of a window, and then neatly returned . . . ; the gracefully finished gable copings; the frequent appearance in gables of date-stones, oval or circular, with initials, elegantly lettered; the abundance of ornamental finials, sometimes carrying balls, sometimes more fanciful forms, as for instance those which suggest flames; the lofty, well-designed chimney stacks crowned with generous cornices: these are all characteristic of the Cotswolds. The most striking feature of the domestic style of this part of England is, however, the great place occupied by the gable. Where other regions used dormer windows, either standing on the wall or set back on the roof, the Cotswold builders carried up the main wall to form a gable, often all but touching its neighbours on either side, and with a ridge as high, or nearly as high, as the main ridge of the roof. And below the gables, especially in moderately-sized or small houses, run those long ranges of rather low windows which are another attractive feature of Cotswold buildings.' There is no monotonous regularity of design and style in a Cotswold village, however, despite the uniformity of material.

Though thatch is sometimes used effectively, the steeply-pitched roof of the traditional Cotswold house is normally of stone slabs, or 'slates' as they are called, somewhat confusingly for the layman. These are obtained from the thinner beds of the oolite, and they are usually hung with the larger slates at the eaves and the smaller ones towards the ridge. Formerly, they were generally hung dry, with oak or deal pegs, but nowadays nails are more often used. A remarkable feature of the Cotswold roof is that in the 'valley', where two roofs join at different angles, the slates are fitted in one piece, with no division between one roof and its neighbour. The stones for the roof cresting, too, are frequently carved out of single blocks.

In the valleys around Stroud, penetrating into the Cotswolds, there are some large villages that owe their size to the broadcloth trade, of which this became an important centre. Many of these developed later than the true Cotswold village, and they show a mingling of building materials, brick and tile, for instance, being used alongside stone, with less satisfying effect. In other regions of the limestone belt, too, except in some of the Northamptonshire and Rutland villages, the high perfection achieved by the Cotswold village will hardly be found.

To the south of the Bristol Avon the limestone belt is not so impressive. Through east Somerset it is mainly seen as a series of scarps and ridges, many of them wooded, and in Dorset it seems to merge imperceptibly into the chalklands (a geologically confusing area this, though its topography is clear). On the east in this region, the Upper Greensand makes its presence felt in some finely wooded ranges, and on the west the lias is more in evidence, both in its effect on the landscape (the country is mostly broken up into a welter of tumbled hills) and in the village building. The honey-coloured liassic Ham Hill stone, beautiful but not very durable, is used intensively round the Somerset–Dorset border. Farther north, there are delightful villages of the golden-hued oolitic Bath stones, but the famous white Portland stone from the promontory which ends the limestone belt has not been employed to any great extent locally. Farther east from here, though, we saw the silver-grey Purbeck limestone in the village of Corfe Castle, on the edge of the chalk country. But over all this region there is not the attention to detail or quality of finish we found in the Cotswolds.

The limestone belt in its extension north-eastward from the Cotswolds also shows some marked variations. Basically, the rock structure is the same; a steep escarpment facing north and west across the Midland Plain, with a long dip slope running down to the claylands of the Cherwell, the Great Ouse and the Nene. But the oolite here has been worn away at the escarpment top to reveal the underlying bed of Middle Lias. This outcrop reaches its most prominent point in Edgehill, on the borders of Warwickshire and Oxfordshire, and in this neighbourhood can be seen some of the broad but shallow quarries of ironstone, a deposit formed from the limestone by percolating water bearing salts of iron in solution. The colour of this stone, varying from a light brown to a deeper, almost orange, shade, is evident in the villages hereabouts, which are mostly of coursed rubble with quoins of ashlar. The lias, though not so good a building stone, was used everywhere instead of oolite in the limestone country where it was easier to obtain. But in the humblest cottage the rubble was well fitted and great care was taken with the stonework of the chimneys, windows and other features, even if the walls were left rough.

When we reach Northamptonshire and Rutland, we are again in a region of rich building stone. The quarries at Barnack, for instance, supplied stone for Peterborough cathedral and for facing the cathedrals of Ely and Norwich, and those at Ketton provided stone for many of the Cambridge colleges, to mention only two of the famous series of quarries that have been worked for centuries. The limestone here, tougher than the Cotswold stone, is mostly a pale grey, toning to a warm-hued buff or pink, though in the northern part of this region, where the Middle Lias marlstone outcrops, as around Rockingham, the ironstone in the deposits tinges it a deep brown.

The scenery of this part of England may not be very exciting, but the villages are an architectural delight. The quoins, jambs and lintels of the houses are invariably of stone, even in the more modest dwellings, and there is a great generosity not only in the details but in the finish. In the churches, too, can be found some of the best building of any period, but especially of the fourteenth century, and spires are almost commonplace. In no other part of the country, in fact, are spires, all of good proportions, scattered so thickly over the landscape as on these gentle pastoral uplands.

The roofs of the houses in this region are sometimes of thatch, though the natural material is the famous Colly Weston stone slate. The slates are usually larger but thinner and lighter than those of the Cotswolds, and they are cut in rather a special way. The stone, which laminates freely, is preferably quarried in the autumn and exposed to the action of frost during the winter. The frost, accentuated by watering the slates each evening, swells the moisture between the laminations and when the thaw sets in, the stone is easily struck into layers with a hammer. The slates are fixed on to the roofs with wooden pegs or (nowadays) copper nails, and then 'torched' or plastered with hair mortar on the under side. So prepared and fitted, they will last for centuries.

Villages of the Limestone Country

(a) South of the Bristol Avon:

ABBOTSBURY (Dt), sheltered in a valley behind the long pebble barrier of Chesil Bank, is on the edge of the limestone spur which leads away southward to Portland. It has a splendid fifteenth-century tithe-barn built of the local ironstone, part of a large Benedictine abbey founded in the eleventh century, other remains of which can be seen in walls and cottages. To the south-west of the village are the Earl of Ilchester's famous swannery and his beautiful sub-tropical gardens.

EAST COKER (Sm), in the angle between the roads from Yeovil to Dorchester and Exeter, is a delightful village among the quiet hills, with many attractive houses. A steep road leads up past a charming park-like green and a row of almshouses, built in stone about 1640, to the fifteenth-century church. This stands in the grounds of Coker Court, like the church built in Ham Hill stone and also of the fifteenth century, but added to at various times; the plain east front is of the eighteenth century.

HINTON ST GEORGE (Sm), north of Crewkerne and west of the road to Ilchester and Ilminster, is a pleasant stone-built village with three roads meeting at the fourteenth-century market cross. One of the roads leads to the fine fifteenth-century church, which has a beautiful pinnacled tower of the characteristic Somerset type, built in 1494. To the south-east of the village extends the large park of Hinton House, which is mostly of the seventeenth and eighteenth centuries.

LACOCK (Wt), in the Avon valley south of Chippenham, is one of the most famous and beautiful villages in England. Its prosperity dates from the growth of the wool industry in this district in the fourteenth and fifteenth centuries. The picturesque streets form a square, with well-preserved houses mostly built in the sixteenth and seventeenth centuries, though a few are earlier and others are

of the eighteenth century. The charming stone houses are diversi-
fied by some fine timber-framed gables and the use of brick here
and there, as in the eighteenth-century front of the Red Lion Inn.
At the end of Church Street is a cruck-built house of the fourteenth
century. Lacock Abbey, near the river, was founded in 1232 as an
Augustinian nunnery and converted after the Reformation into
a mansion which was attractively Gothicised in the eighteenth
century. The Abbey and most of the village now belong to the
National Trust.

MELLS (Sm), in the wooded Wadbury valley west of Frome, was
called by Leland 'a praty townelet of clothing'. It is a scattered
village with many attractive stone houses, the oldest and most
interesting being the terraces of tiny cottages in New Street built
as early as 1470 by Abbot Selwood. The High Street climbs past
the end of this street to the gates of the fine church with its
early-sixteenth-century tower, facing across neatly trimmed
hedges to the gabled stone manor house (Elizabethan, but much
restored).

MONTACUTE (Sm) is built mainly along the winding Yeovil–Ilminster
road under Ham Hill (or Hamdon Hill), which provided the stone
for its warm-coloured cottages. The lane past the seventeenth-
century gate to the church (itself mainly of the fourteenth to
fifteenth centuries) ends at the fifteenth-century Priory gatehouse.
There are seventeenth- to eighteenth-century houses in the
pleasant square called The Borough, and close by is the entrance
to the lovely Elizabethan mansion of Montacute House, built in
1588–1600 of the Ham Hill stone and with a beautiful contemporary
garden.

NORTON ST PHILIP (Sm) is on the road from Trowbridge to Radstock
in the pleasantly hilly country south of Bath. The tower and much
of the body of the church date from the mid-seventeenth century.
The finest of the several interesting buildings is the fifteenth-
century George Inn, one of the most fascinating medieval hostelries
in England, built originally by the priors of Hinton for use as a
staple house. The long, low front of the ground floor is of stone,
with richly carved bow-windows, and above rise two timber-
framed storeys, both overhanging and the lower having oriel
windows.

QUEEN CAMEL (Sm) is an exceptionally well-kept village on the road
from Yeovil to Castle Cary, below the face of the limestone hills. It
consists mainly of one long street with many charming stone cottages
fronted by flower-filled gardens. A stone-paved causeway leads
round a wall enriched with ornamental piers and then between
rows of cottages to the fine fourteenth- to fifteenth-century
church with its tall tower. The first part of the name is derived
from Queen Eleanor, who was given the property by Edward I
before 1280.

STEEPLE ASHTON (Wt) is in rising country of the limestone east of the
Warminster–Chippenham road, below the north edge of Salisbury
Plain, and shows the contrast between the stone and the chalk.
A dignified village, once a centre of the wool industry, it takes the
first part of its name from its staple or market. The sixteenth-
century and other houses of stone, brick and timberwork are
grouped round the market cross, with the beautifully carved
tower of the late-fifteenth-century church rising above the roofs.

STOKE-SUB-HAMDON (Sm), called Stoke-under-Ham locally, is on the
Yeovil–Ilminster road right under Ham Hill, from which it
quarried the beautiful liassic stone for its charming cottages. The
village is really in two distinct parts: East Stoke, where there is a
church of great interest, mostly of the thirteenth and fourteenth
centuries; and West Stoke, the larger part, with seventeenth- and
eighteenth-century houses and the remarkable fifteenth-century
Priory, in reality formerly a chantry house.

STOURTON (Wt), south of Frome and east of Bruton, is actually on the
greensand between the limestone and the south-westward extension of Salisbury Plain. One of the most charmingly situated
villages in Wiltshire, it lies in a sheltered wooded dell. A road
leads down past a long stone building, now the village hall, to a
green shaded by tall beeches. On the north the village is enclosed
by the enchantingly landscaped gardens of the eighteenth-century
mansion of Stourhead.

TINTINHULL (Sm) lies among orchards, south of the Ilchester–Ilminster
road and north of the limestone hills which rise above Montacute.
Tintinhull Court dates mostly from the early seventeenth century,
but has fifteenth-century portions; Tintinhull House is a delightful
manor house of about 1700 with a lovely formal garden; and there

28 *Hinton St George, Somerset*

are other good houses in this charmingly retired village. The thirteenth-century church has a tower with fifteenth-century details.

(b) *The Cotswolds:*

BIBURY (Gl), on the Cirencester–Burford road, in the little valley of the Coln, has several groups of stone cottages in the characteristic Cotswold style. The most notable of these is Arlington Row, a terrace of early-seventeenth-century dormered and gabled cottages, once a wool factory, facing the southern end of a long meadow called Rack Isle where the wool used to be hung on racks to dry. At the northern end is the Swan Inn, facing across delightful gardens to the solid-looking millhouse; and there are fine cottages in the square near the church and the early-seventeenth-century Bibury Court.

BIDDESTONE (Wt) is an airy upland village between the roads from Chippenham to Bristol and Bath. Unlike the valley villages in this region, it has had room to develop, and the pleasant grey stone houses, some of which are of the eighteenth century, spread themselves casually round an extensive green with a pond. This is a village to see in high summer, when the better-known Bibury, Bourton-on-the-Water, Broadway and Castle Combe are too congested for their proper enjoyment.

BOURTON-ON-THE-HILL (Gl) is indeed on the hill. The attractive village climbs up a steep slope mounted by the road between Moreton-in-Marsh and Broadway. The typical stone cottages are set back behind little gardens and stone walls hung with aubrietia and other plants that flourish in the Cotswold soil, and the fourteenth- to fifteenth-century church takes its place naturally among them. Near Bourton House, at the foot of the village, is a fine old tithe barn of the late sixteenth century.

BOURTON-ON-THE-WATER (Gl), lying just off the road from Cirencester to Stow-on-the-Wold, is a stone-built village mainly of one long street with a green divided by the Windrush, which is crossed by some charming little bridges. Though normally one of the pleasantest of the Cotswold villages, it has not been improved by having become a favourite week-end resort of motorists and coach-trippers. Among the attractions it now offers are a Witch-

29 *Bourton-on-the-Water, Gloucestershire*
30 *Steeple Ashton, Wiltshire*

craft Museum, a Birdland Museum and a scale model of the village, laid out by the landlord behind the Old New Inn.

BROADWAY (Wo), though one of the most charming villages in England, is unfortunately almost too accessible and too well known. It lies on the lower slopes of the Cotswold escarpment, on the main road from Oxford to Worcester, and its wide sloping street is lined with genial yellow-brown stone-built and stone-roofed houses of the sixteenth and seventeenth centuries, among them the imposing seventeenth-century Lygon Arms. To see these, it is worth facing the crowds in summer, for Broadway is architecturally more consistent and satisfying than Bourton-on-the-Water, on the other side of the Cotswolds. Near the village green is the Abbot's Grange, a fourteenth-century house of the abbots of Pershore.

BURFORD (Ox) will claim with justification that it is a town, but for me it still has the atmosphere of a village and it is altogether much too good to miss. The delightful main street, descending a steep hill to the Windrush, has a wealth of stone (and some brick) houses and inns of many styles and periods, but mostly of the sixteenth to eighteenth centuries, though the Market Hall, or Tolsey (tolls were paid here), is basically a fifteenth-century building. To the right at the foot of the hill is the exceptionally interesting church, chiefly of the thirteenth and fifteenth centuries, with a prominent stone spire.

CASTLE COMBE (Wt) stakes a high claim to be the most perfect village in the Cotswolds, if not in England. It lies north of the Chippenham–Bristol road, and the approach to it could hardly be improved. The village, nestling in the deep wooded ravine of the By Brook, a tributary of the Avon, is gathered irregularly round its thirteenth-century market cross, which is placed under a fine timber roof supported by massive stone piers. Castle Combe has a pleasing thirteenth- to fifteenth-century church, but the chief interest is in the houses themselves, which are quite unspoilt. Of varying styles and periods, with their walls of soft brownish stone or cream colour-wash and their moss-grown roofs of grey-brown stone slates, they are exceptionally harmonious; every group of cottages makes a picture and every prospect is a delight in this secluded village, backed everywhere by thickly wooded hill slopes.

ILMINGTON (Wa), on the extreme northern slopes of the Cotswolds, between the roads from Stratford to Shipston-on-Stour and Broadway, is a large, rambling village, beautifully situated and pleasant in itself, its stone houses roofed with excellent thatch or stone-slates. The church shows work of all the periods from the twelfth to the sixteenth centuries. The rectory, to the north, is a fine stone-built house of the sixteenth to seventeenth centuries; the manor house, a little east of the church, is a many-gabled building of about 1500, since enlarged.

LOWER SLAUGHTER (Gl), on the other side of the main road from Bourton-on-the-Water, is quite different in temperament. It is a fascinating little village bisected by a branch of the Windrush. The limpid stream, crossed by many stone or timber bridges, is separated from the irregular lines of characteristic Cotswold cottages by strips of green shaded with beech and other trees. Lower Slaughter, like other secluded villages in this region, is gaining favour as a place for retirement.

MINSTER LOVELL (Ox), charmingly situated on the north bank of the Windrush below and away from the busy Oxford–Cheltenham road, is a pretty little 'dead-end' village of stone-built cottages, some of them with thatched roofs indicating the proximity of the clay country. The delightful Swan Inn, however, has a roof of Stonesfield slates. The cruciform church, built about 1450 by Lord William Lovell, has hardly been touched since; behind it are the ruins of the once-moated manor house, built by the Lovells in the first half of the fifteenth century.

SAINTBURY (Gl), architecturally one of the most satisfying of the smaller Cotswold villages, is built up the escarpment face, above the road from Broadway to Stratford. Its lovely clusters of stone-roofed and grey-walled cottages, separated by wide strips of green, show a surprising richness of craftmanship and wealth of decoration. At the bottom of the hill is the fourteenth-century village cross, and at the top of the village is the pretty little church, which is partly Norman.

SHERSTON MAGNA (Wt), on the road from Malmesbury to Chipping Sodbury, stands high on a plateau above the infant Avon, in a less-frequented part of the Cotswolds. This peaceful village has an exceptionally wide main street of grey stone and colour-washed houses and inns, the prospect closed at the northern end by the great tower of the church, built in 1730 and a genuine Gothic survival.

SNOWSHILL (Gl), in a fold of the escarpment face south of Broadway, embowered in trees, is one of the most beautifully situated Cotswold villages, with an engaging assortment of houses in the warm-hued limestone. The centre of the former village green is occupied by the church, unfortunately rebuilt in rather a harsh Victorian Gothic style in 1864. Snowshill Manor, on the crest of the hill, is an unspoilt sixteenth-century Cotswold house with a handsome early-eighteenth-century front and a lovely terraced garden.

STANTON (Gl), east of the road between Broadway and Winchcomb, is a charming village of dignified stone cottages of the sixteenth to seventeenth centuries. These make a graceful sweep round a bend of its by-road before beginning the climb up the wooded escarpment, from which there is a view of Bredon Hill and the Malverns. Some of the houses show their Gothic roots in windows with arches arranged in arcades, and timber-framed barns indicate the closeness of the once thickly-forested Midland Plain. Stanton Court, at the foot of the village, is a delightful late-sixteenth-century house.

STANWAY (Gl), though hardly a mile and a half from Stanton, differs from its sister village in several respects. It lies just off a main road, for instance (that from Stow-on-the-Wold to Tewkesbury), and it has a fine early-sixteenth-century manor house with an imposing Renaissance gatehouse (attributed to Inigo Jones), which with the fourteenth-century church and contemporary tithe-barn makes an exquisite group. If one of the smallest, this is certainly one of the most attractive of the Cotswold villages.

(c) *North-East of the Cotswolds:*

ADDERBURY (Ox), mostly lying west of the Oxford–Banbury road, is a large village with many attractive old houses, including the seventeenth-century Adderbury House, west of the green, where the poet Earl of Rochester lived. The noble cruciform church of the fourteenth and fifteenth centuries has a tower and spire, 150 feet high, of about 1300. To the north of it are the rectory and

tithe-barn built in the fourteenth century by Bishop William of
Wykeham, the builder of much of Winchester cathedral.

ASHBY ST LEDGERS (Np) is a quiet village between Daventry and Rugby,
to the west of (and fortunately secluded from) the A5 and the
M1. It has many stone-built cottages, the newer ones harmonising
with the old. At the end of the single street are the entrances to the
fourteenth- to fifteenth-century church and (through a stone
porch-house with a timber-framed upper storey) to the restored
sixteenth- to seventeenth-century manor house of the Catesbys, a
meeting place of the Gunpowder Plot conspirators.

AYNHO (Np), on the Aylesbury–Banbury road, is an enchanting
village crowning a hill above the Cherwell, remarkable especially
for the apricots growing on its stone cottage walls. Part of the
village, which has sixteenth-century and later houses, is looped
off the main road, to the north. On the south opens a view of the
charming house of Aynhoe Park; rebuilt in the seventeenth
century, it was altered by Thomas Archer in 1707-14 and again by
Sir John Soane in 1800-5. The Dower House was formerly
occupied by the grammar school, founded in 1654.

BARNWELL (Np), south of Oundle and east of the Nene, is a delightfully planned village, its stone-built houses mostly bordering the
stream and forming a semicircle round the fine church, whose
thirteenth- to fourteenth-century tower and broach spire rise
from an embankment. To the north, in the grounds of Barnwell Manor, the country home of the Duke of Gloucester, are
the huge round bastions of the castle, an example of the Edwardian-
style fortress, but dating from as early as 1266.

BELTON (Rt), which lies in quiet, pastoral country north of the Leicester–Uppingham road, is a very attractive village with ironstone
cottages of the seventeenth century and later, grouped round the
rise on which stands the low-built church, also of ironstone but
with a limestone tower of the fourteenth century. Notable to the
west of the church are the early-seventeenth-century Old Hall and
the early-eighteenth-century Westbourne House; this is also of
ironstone, but has limestone facings.

BLOXHAM (Ox), on the road from Banbury to Chipping Norton, is a
very pleasant village, its houses chiefly in the local ironstone, with
thatched roofs. It is dominated by the splendid church, mainly

built about 1300 except for the richly-decorated late-fourteenth-century tower and spire, 198 feet high, with a fine west doorway; a thirteenth-century south porch with two priests' rooms over, an unusual arrangement; and a noble fifteenth-century chapel, also on the south.

COLLY WESTON (Np), on the Kettering road south-west of Stamford, has been famous for its limestone roofing slates since the fourteenth century. The village itself is worthy of this great tradition; its pleasing street of well-built houses, some of the seventeenth century, with roofs of the local slates and a wealth of bow and dormer windows, slopes down from the church, which is mostly of the fifteenth century (including the sturdy tower), to the seventeenth-century bridge over the Welland.

DUDDINGTON (Np), only a mile from Colly Weston along the Kettering road, where this is crossed by the Peterborough–Uppingham road, is another lovely limestone village. It has a church mainly of the twelfth to thirteenth centuries with a broach spire (spoiled only by the nineteenth-century chancel), a seventeenth-century Manor House likewise altered in the nineteenth century, and a street of eighteenth-century houses winding down to the bridge, which is basically of the fourteenth century, and a fine watermill of 1664 on the Welland.

EXTON (Rt), between the roads from Stamford to Oakham and Grantham, has many delightful cottages, some of them with thatched roofs, round the tree-shaded green and in the near-by lanes. The church, largely rebuilt in 1846 except for the tall and unusual fourteenth-century steeple, stands apart, in the pleasant park of Exton Hall, which was newly built in the first half of the nineteenth century in a Victorian Tudor style. To the east of the church are the ruins of the old hall, burnt down in 1810.

GEDDINGTON (Np), north-east of Kettering on the road to Stamford, was once a royal manor. A narrow thirteenth-century bridge crosses the little river Ise to a small square in the centre of which rises a beautifully-sculptured Eleanor Cross, one of the three remaining of the 11 erected shortly after 1294 to mark the resting places on the last journey of Eleanor of Castile, queen of Edward I, who died at Harby in Lincolnshire in 1290. Beyond the square is the interesting church, which has a characteristic fourteenth-century tower and spire.

GREAT TEW (Ox) is a small village of singular loveliness south of the Banbury–Chipping Norton road, on the slope above a wooded valley. Its thatched and stone-roofed yellow-brown cottages, with mullioned windows and charming gardens, climb along one side of a green, in a setting of fine old trees. The lofty church, mainly of the thirteenth to fifteenth centuries, stands farther up the hill, in the grounds of the rebuilt manor house of the Falklands.

HALLATON (Le), in the ironstone belt of the Middle Lias, some distance south of the Leicester–Uppingham road, is a very attractive village with houses of the seventeenth and eighteenth centuries, of brick and stone, some of the latter having thatched roofs, gathered round an unusual cross which has a curious conical top. The impressive twelfth- to thirteenth-century church, to the south-west, has a handsome tower, unusually detailed for this period.

KETTON (Rt), on the Stamford–Uppingham road and on the opposite side of the Welland from Colly Weston, was long famous for its stone and is now well known for cement. The village has many excellent houses in its grey limestone and an exceptionally fine church, built between 1190 and 1250, with an impressive west front. To this was added the magnificent fourteenth-century tower and broach spire, constructed, however, of Barnack stone, not the local stone. Opposite the churchyard is a sixteenth- to eighteenth-century building called The Priory.

LYDDINGTON (Rt), or Liddington, between the Uppingham–Kettering road and the Welland, is a quiet village mainly of one street, with very many seventeenth- and eighteenth-century houses built of the local brown stone. On one side is the interesting church, rebuilt (except for the fourteenth-century tower) late in the fifteenth century, but with a chancel added in 1635. To the north of it is the restored Bede-House, originally built as a manor house by John Russell, bishop of Lincoln in 1480-95, but converted into a hospital in 1602 by Thomas, Lord Burghley.

ROCKINGHAM (Np) is a dignified village on the Uppingham–Kettering road as it climbs steeply above the Welland. The wide grass-bordered road is lined with seventeenth- and eighteenth-century houses built of ironstone, with roofs of thatch or Colly Weston

slate. At the top of the hill is the great Norman gateway of Rockingham Castle, a royal possession from the time of William the
Conqueror to that of Elizabeth I. As it stands, it is largely Elizabethan, though built within the Norman wall and with a charming
rose garden on the site of the Norman keep.

WROXTON (Ox), west of the point where the Banbury–Stratford road
crosses the deep valley of the Sor Brook, is a village of characteristic brown-stone cottages with thatched and stone-slate roofs.
The church is an interesting fourteenth-century building with a
tower recast in 1747 and monuments of the Pope and North
families, the owners of Wroxton Abbey, to the south, a delightful
early-seventeenth-century house, with many gables and mullioned
windows, on the site of an Augustinian priory.

8 South-West England

The area covered by this section is the whole of Devon and Cornwall
and all that part of Somerset lying west of the limestone formations. So
far, we have found that the type of village building we have met with has
been dictated very largely by the geological pattern, and I could have
continued with this plan based on the rock formations. But the whole
of the south-west of England is so complex that it would have been
impossible to divide it up adequately in the amount of space I have
available. To impose such a plan on this region would have made it too
complicated for a superficial survey like this, and, in any case, it would
have been somewhat misleading. The pattern of building, as we shall
find again in the north, does not always follow rigorously that of the
geological formations.

In the south-west, the geographical pattern is equally as important
as the geological. Nowhere else in England (except perhaps in the Lake
District and parts of the Pennines) are we so aware of the general
subordination of building to landscape. Here, if anywhere, the villager
has cause to feel overshadowed by the landscape, and may seem to have
shaped his habitations to fit in with it. Unlike his fellows of East
Anglia or the Cotswolds, the village builder appears not to have
intended to make something architecturally satisfying, but to adapt
himself as simply as possible to the forms already created by nature.
No art, in truth, appears to have made the villages of the south-west

except that of filling in unobtrusively a few crannies and niches in the valleys and the folds of the hills or coast, taking advantage of the very complexity of the landscape.

The northern half of Somerset, in particular—between say the Bristol Avon and the Quantock Hills—encompasses a greater variety of landscape than almost any other area of similar size in England. Ranges of hills appear to spread out haphazardly in every direction, rivers to flow in some places in open, level valleys, in others in narrow, winding ravines. This complicated pattern is the result of the great diversity of rock formations that are present in this area—outcrops of practically every group of the English rocks are to be seen—combined with the immense amount of movement that has taken place since the strata were laid down.

The great complexity in the rock structure in north Somerset displays itself, too, in the extent of the materials used in village building: apart from timber, we find stone, brick and cob in turn as we move westward. Most of the houses and cottages owe their colour and style to the rocks found in their particular localities, though the churches, with their splendid and distinctive towers, a feature of this part of the country, are invariably built of limestone from the oolite formations.

The limestone, as if to confuse the pattern, throws forward several outliers to the west of its escarpment (to be geologically exact, they are detached ridges left by the weathering back of the escarpment face). Dundry Hill, south of Bristol, well known for its building stone, is one of these. But the most prominent of the ranges in this region, effectively splitting it in half, is that of the Mendip Hills, a long plateau of Carboniferous Limestone, a formation we shall see much of in the north, and which is not of course to be confused with the oolitic limestone. The plateau rises to between 800 and 1,000 feet and is bounded by grey crags enclosing dry ravines of which Cheddar Gorge is the most famous. The stone has not been used much for building, and there are no settlements of any size on the almost level uplands, which are exposed and bare toward their seaward end. All the villages are gathered round the flanks of the hills, on a narrow margin where springs rise at the foot of the porous limestone, between the steep slopes and the lower country that surrounds the Mendips.

The richly undulating country between the Mendips and the

Bristol Avon is split up by many valleys. Here we see outcrops of the formations known collectively as the New Red Sandstone, a more prominent feature in the Western Marches and the Midland Plain, though the colours in Somerset are just as bright and varied. In this region, geologically confusing though otherwise most pleasant, the red marls, lias clays and limestones show themselves in the village buildings. To the south of the Mendips stretches a level plain—the Somerset 'moors'—broken only by the solitary knoll of Glastonbury Tor and the low range of the Polden Hills. In this broad, flat, green fenland, where silt and peat are much in evidence, settlements are few and poor (the churches built chiefly of blue lias are the most noticeable feature), but farther south and west the red marls make themselves conspicuous, extending past the Quantocks to the fringes of Exmoor and the Vale of Taunton Deane, a fertile tract famous for its orchards, where the villages are more flourishing and more numerous. The type of pantile first made at Bridgwater in the eighteenth century is a feature of the buildings in this quarter of Somerset.

The narrow but striking range of the Quantocks, rising abruptly to over 1,000 feet above the sea, is a huge outlier of the Old Red Sandstone that makes up most of the structure of Exmoor, Cornwall and South Devon. The western slopes of the hills are steep and thickly wooded, but the eastern side is penetrated by several of the lovely combes that are characteristic of the south-west. Some of the delightful Quantock villages nestle in these quiet valleys, though the majority, as in the Mendips, are situated where the hill slopes reach the surrounding plain.

Devon and Cornwall with west Somerset, perhaps the most favoured and certainly the most popular region in England, seem to be cut off from the rest of the country; this segregation makes itself felt not only in the customs and scenery, but in the character of the villages as well. The reason may be found partly in the fact that this great promontory was long remote from the main events in England, partly perhaps in the proximity of the sea and the moors (neither of which ever seem very far away), but also to some extent in the geological structure. The boundary is really a band of the New Red Sandstone that runs right across Somerset and Devon from Minehead and the margin of the Brendon Hills to Exeter, the Teign estuary and Tor Bay. It forms a division between the lias and limestone of the country south of Bath and the greensand of the Blackdown Hills, on the east, and the older Red Sandstones and Carboniferous formations farther west.

The New Red Sandstone, as we shall find in the Western Marches, is not in general a good material for building, though there are some satisfactory stones. For houses, preference has usually been given to bricks made from the rich red marls found in conjunction with the sandstone. The villages, like the landscape of this region, are very colourful, with a delightful mingling of reds, greys and greens in their building; and church towers here, too, are a particular feature. At Beer, on the coast between the Axe and the Exe, there is a singular outcrop of chalk (it is almost a chalky limestone in texture) which was quarried for Exeter cathedral in the fourteenth century and for churches over a wide area of Devon and Dorset from the fifteenth century. It was especially useful as a freestone and had the further advantage that it could be carried by sea.

The Old Red Sandstone, sometimes called the Devonian series because it is most familiar in this county, has other deposits beside sandstones in its composition. There is a certain amount of limestone, and also of slate, which has been made use of in various ways in village building. Slate is quarried from the Brendon Hills, among numerous places, and it may have been the popularity of slates from here that first led to the unfortunate invasion of the cheaper Welsh slates early in the nineteenth century. Slate-stone has been used extensively in Cornwall for building, as we shall see, and slates are employed in every part of the south-west for roofing. A speciality of this region is the covering of house fronts with slate; this was particularly favoured in south Devon and east Cornwall during the eighteenth and early nineteenth centuries. The slates were often hung on timber-framed buildings and it seems most likely that the original intention was simply to cover the lath and plaster with an impervious material. But slate-hanging was also adopted for walls of brick, slate-stone or even granite, and its later application was more often than not decorative: intricate patterns were formed with the slates and these were sometimes shaped to give a better decorative effect, like the tiles we saw in the Weald. The slates are usually fixed with pegs into wooden battens, except on brick walls, when they can be nailed into the mortar.

The 'West Country', though an immensely varied region, is best loved for its rugged and imposing coast scenery. On the north, except around the mouths of the Taw and the Torridge, the cliffs run high and uninterrupted for many miles and habitations are necessarily few. For some distance, these cliffs are the northward termination of Exmoor, a vast expanse of swelling, bracken-covered moorland, much of it over 1,400 feet above the sea. Round its borders, the pastures often reach up to over 1,000 feet, as well as stretching up the valleys, but these are frequently too narrow or too densely wooded for cultivation on any large scale. In consequence, there are many scattered farmsteads in the valleys but comparatively few village settlements, and hardly any at all on the moor itself.

The central part of Devon, between Exmoor and Dartmoor, is a region of Gritstone formations, mostly consisting of sandstones and dark shales, and not at all like those of the Pennines we shall meet later. Known as the Culm Measures, they are well seen where they reach the sea in the wide Barnstaple Bay. Inland, in the undulating, green and fertile country, are many quiet and unspoilt villages, reached by charming lanes between high banks. The local stone, hard, rough and rather sombre, has been used here to a certain extent, though granite is preferred as we near Dartmoor.

Dartmoor is a great mass of wild, high-lying moorland, treeless and barren, its dark tracts of peat dotted with grey granite tors. As might be expected, there are hardly any settlements on this waste, apart from a few scattered farmsteads (though it was popular with pre-historic man). The borders of the moor, however, are carved with delectable little combes, hidden away in which, here and there, will be found a pleasing variety of small villages. In many of these, the cottages, and even the churches, are constructed of 'moorstones', huge rectangular blocks of granite brought down from the moor. They are in fact to be seen in solid, unpretentious houses and churches over a wide area round Dartmoor. Grey in colour and coarse in texture, these great blocks are not easily shaped and do not yield themselves to decoration, but they well express the basic simplicity of life around the moor.

The walls of the older cottages in Devon and west Somerset, away from the moorland influence, are mostly of 'cob', which consists basically of mud, mixed with chopped straw, chalk, gravel, pebbles, broken slate, sand and whatever was available, and with lime to make

31 *Mevagissey, Cornwall*

it set. Cob construction has been known here since the thirteenth century, and this region can still boast more cob cottages than any other, many of them surviving from the sixteenth and seventeenth centuries. To keep out the damp from above and below, the cob needed an effective foundation and an overhanging roof. To quote an old Devon saying, 'All cob wants is a good hat and a good pair of shoes'. The foundation was usually of stone, sometimes of pebbles; on top of this the cob was laid in layers, usually about two but sometimes as much as four feet wide and about a foot thick. It was laid wet and soft, then trodden down and left for a week or more to dry out before the next layer was put down. In this way, it might take two years to build a two-storeyed house. The outside was finished off with a coat of whitewash or colour wash (cream, buff or pink was preferred) and in later buildings it was probably covered with plaster or cement, if not both. The invariable roofing material for a cob building was thatch, with generous overhanging eaves; the chimney-stacks were of brick, and the ovens were often set in little round projections.

The south coast of Devon, at least from Tor Bay westward, is nearly as rock-bound as the north, but the cliffs are neither so high nor so precipitous; they are dissected by numerous very beautiful inlets, cutting deep into the inland plateau, and many delightful small villages will be found along their shores. The dark, rugged cliffs, made up of grits and hard shales, with igneous rocks such as granite showing out in places, extend westward into Cornwall, where most of the coastal villages grew up as fishing settlements on tiny, almost land-locked bays, though they are now dependent more on the holiday industry.

The fishing village was in fact a new form of settlement that came into being in the fourteenth and fifteenth centuries, no doubt because of some change in fishing methods that allowed whole villages to obtain a living from it. In Cornwall, the name of Polperro is first recorded in 1303, Penzance in 1332, Padstow in 1351, St Ives in 1377, Bude in 1400 and Mevagissey in 1410, to pick out only a few of these new villages. Lynmouth, in north Devon, is mentioned in 1330, but Clovelly was apparently founded in the sixteenth century, slightly later than most of the others.

The characteristic Cornish fishing village is a picturesque jumble of cottages usually built of massive granite or sandstone blocks from the

32 *Zennor, Cornwall*
33 *Abbotsbury, Dorset*

uplands, their simple, straightforward character matching the rather unrelenting material. The slate-stone I mentioned in Devon is also employed extensively in eastern Cornwall. The roofing of the older houses is invariably of slate, which has been in use here, as in the Lake District, from very early times. Fine-grained 'blue' slates from Delabole, near Camelford, which has the largest slate quarry in England, are in great demand, though the colour is a sombre grey rather than blue. But what these Cornish villages lack in colour is more than compensated for by the rich reddish-brown cliffs backed by a seascape of variegated blues and greens.

Little villages also seclude themselves in the many valleys that run inland, but there are few on the barren windswept uplands. A series of granite intrusions runs along the backbone of Cornwall, and where these reach the sea, as they do in the Land's End peninsula, the cliffs are high and steep, and the tiny villages, built entirely of the native granite, are confined to the few sandy coves. The Lizard peninsula has rather a different complexity: its rugged cliffs and enchanting little coves are fashioned to a great extent from serpentine, a magnesium silicate 'marble' which gives them their lovely green and purple tones. This stone, once popular for architectural ornamentation, has been used extensively in the local building; it has the advantage of being very durable and easily worked, though the villages tend to have a somewhat uniform green hue.

Villages of South-West England

(a) North Devon and West Somerset

BOSSINGTON (Sm) is a secluded and luxuriantly verdant village, with flowery gardens and fine walnut and other trees, and numerous delightful cottages, many of them whitewashed. It lies north-east of Porlock, on the Horner Water, about $\frac{1}{2}$-mile inland from Porlock Bay, and at the foot of Selworthy Beacon, from which there are wonderful views across the valley to Exmoor and over the Bristol Channel to the mountains of South Wales. Bossington, like Selworthy, is part of the large Holnicote Estate that now belongs to the National Trust.

CLOVELLY (Dv) is certainly the loveliest village in Devon and manages to remain quite unspoilt. This enchanting fishing village is beautifully and indeed uniquely situated in a narrow cleft of the cliffs, facing out across Barnstaple Bay. The cobbled street, too pre-cipitous for wheeled traffic, descends in steps for some 400 feet to the little cove with its curved pier that forms a miniature harbour at the foot of the cliffs. The whitewashed flower-decked houses are all huddled on ledges at different levels, a considerable achievement in village building, and the whole is embossed in dense woods. Perhaps the most fascinating view of all is that from the sea.

CROSCOMBE (Sm) nestles in a delightful valley under the southern face of the Mendip Hills, between Wells and Shepton Mallet. This very attractive village has a noble fifteenth- and sixteenth-century church rich in Jacobean woodwork and with one of the few spires in Somerset. Among the many interesting houses are the Manor House on the main road south-west of the church, the Old Manor House at the east end of the village—both early Tudor buildings—and the Baptist Chapel, in the fifteenth-century style and formerly the chapel of the manor house.

DUNSTER (Sm) is an entrancing village south of the Minehead–Taunton road. In the broad market place are the quaint octagonal Yarn Market, built in 1609, and the Luttrell Arms Hotel, an interesting house, partly timber-framed, built as a residence about 1500 by the abbots of Cleeve but altered in the early seventeenth century. The market place looks north to the eighteenth-century tower on Conygar Hill, south to the splendid and dominating Castle, bought by the Luttrells in 1376 and showing work of the thirteenth to eighteenth centuries; it is entered by a fifteenth-century gatehouse. The main street leads below the castle, passing The Nunnery—a range of three-storey houses, partly of the fourteenth century, with a remarkable slate-hung front—and leading to the interesting red sandstone Priory Church, of Norman origin but mostly of the fifteenth century.

LYNMOUTH (Dv), a favourite summer resort, and suffering then in consequence, is on the coast between Minehead and Ilfracombe, at the place where the combined waters of the East and West Lyn, after having penetrated deep, wood-filled valleys, push their way through steep banks to the sea. The street leads past houses overhanging the river to the quay and the stone pier or cobb, from which a pretty and much-photographed terrace of cottages begins the ascent of Mars Hill. Around the harbour are some mid-nineteenth-century houses, and newer houses have climbed the hills where they can get a foothold. The havoc wrought by the appalling and tragic floods in 1952 has been carefully repaired.

MUCHELNEY (Sm), in level country south of Langport on the Taunton–Wincanton road, is a pleasant village set among orchards. Its houses, mostly of the seventeenth and eighteenth centuries, incorporate fragments of the Benedictine Abbey, of Saxon foundation, of which other remains, mainly of the fifteenth and early sixteenth centuries, include the abbot's lodging and part of the claustral buildings. In the square to the north is the village cross, partly medieval, and to the north-east is the delightful late-medieval Priest's House.

NETHER STOWEY (Sm) is on the Bridgwater–Minehead road below the east face of the Quantock Hills. Coleridge Cottage, at the west end, was rented by the poet in 1797–1800; here he wrote *The Ancient Mariner* and was joined by Wordsworth in the companionship that resulted in the *Lyrical Ballads*. The village has some houses of the late eighteenth and nineteenth centuries; more elaborate are the fifteenth- and sixteenth-century Stowey Court and the eighteenth-century Poole's House at the east end.

PORLOCK (Sm) is a delightful village on the Minehead–Lynton road at the foot of the notorious Porlock Hill. Though once a port (the name means 'enclosure by the harbour'), it is now a mile from the sea at Porlock Bay. The thirteenth- to fourteenth-century church has a low tower with a shingled spire; the best of the old houses are west of this, around the Ship Inn, where Southey is supposed to have written his lines on Porlock's 'verdant vale'. There are other pretty whitewashed cottages by the harbour at PORLOCK WEIR, a mile and a half to the west.

SAMPFORD COURTENAY (Dv) is in quiet country some distance north of Okehampton and the northern fringe of Dartmoor, between the valley of the upper Taw and that of the Okement, a tributary of the Torridge. The charming village is of particular interest for its noble church, which is mainly of the fifteenth century and contains in its fabric both granite ashlar blocks and also polyphant, an uncommon dark grey-green stone from east Cornwall.

SELWORTHY (Sm) is an enchanting little village on the Holnicote
Estate (page 148), nestling below a wooded fold in the hills at the
foot of Selworthy Beacon. It lies north of the Minehead–Porlock
road and is approached through a tunnel-like avenue. The charming thatched and whitewashed cottages climb a steep little glen
to the fourteenth-century tithe-barn and the surprisingly elaborate
church, mainly of the fifteenth century, but with a fourteenth-
century tower.

STOGUMBER (Sm) lies in a remote valley between the Quantocks and
the Brendon Hills, several miles west of the Taunton–Minehead
road. Steep and narrow streets, with many attractive colour-
washed stone houses, lead up to the little square in front of the
church, a large and quite lavish structure of the fourteenth and
fifteenth centuries with a red sandstone tower, which crowns the
hilltop. In the main street to the south-west are the seventeenth-
century almshouses.

(b) South Devon and Cornwall

AXMOUTH (Dv) is no longer at the mouth of the Axe, though it must
have been at one time (it has a Harbour Inn and a Ship Inn). The
village lies inland from Seaton, on the east side of the wide valley,
and its street of well-cared-for thatched stone and cob cottages,
descending a hill, is followed by a stream over which the approaches
to the cottages are by stone slabs. Some of the best houses face
the church, which has Norman walling in the nave and chancel,
but is mostly of the fifteenth century.

BRANSCOMBE (Dv) straggles down a charming steep-sided valley
between Beer Head and Sidmouth, its thatched and flower-
strewn cottages mostly lying inland and sheltered from the sea.
The excellent cruciform church, at the upper end of the village,
belonged to the Benedictines of St Peter's, Exeter; it has a Norman
tower and nave, but is otherwise of the thirteenth and fourteenth
centuries. Opposite the church is a sixteenth-century building of
unknown origin, possibly the church house.

BROADHEMBURY (Dv) lies north of the Honiton–Tiverton road, in the
depths of a valley under the steep greensand slopes of Black
Down. It is an old-fashioned village with a fifteenth- to sixteenth-
century inn and with buff-washed cottages of thatch and cob

lining the street leading to the little square in front of the church,
which is partly of the fourteenth century but has a handsome
fifteenth-century tower.

CADGWITH (Co), on the east side of the Lizard peninsula, is an exceptionally picturesque little fishing village, scarcely more than a
hamlet in fact, set in a delightful rock-bound sandy cove forming a
tiny natural harbour. The view down from the cliffs is full of
charm: the cottages are dispersed on little ledges in the sides of the
cove, and the brightly-painted boats hauled up on the beach and
the round fishing baskets scattered about combine to make a
characteristically Cornish scene.

COCKINGTON (Dv), though now on the western outskirts of Torquay,
has been well preserved by the municipal authorities. This still
secluded village is famous for its thatched cottages, of which the
best is the Old Forge, while the Drum Inn, built by Sir Edwin
Lutyens in 1934, with its tall thatched roof, fits into the picture.
Higher up are Cockington Court, a sixteenth- to eighteenth-
century manor house with delightful gardens, and the fifteenth-
century red sandstone church.

DITTISHAM (Dv), between Dartmouth and Totnes, is exquisitely placed
on the slopes of a promontory round which the Dart, having
widened out into its long estuary, winds below charmingly wooded
banks. A steep street ascends from the quay (where a ferry
crosses to the Brixham road) to the grey tower of the fourteenth-
to fifteenth-century church, and from this another street of
colour-washed houses drops down on the other side of the promontory towards the estuary again.

DREWSTEIGNTON (Dv) is south of the Exeter–Okehampton road and
stands nearly 700 feet up on a ridge above the wooded upper
valley of the Teign, with a wide prospect all round. Fronting the
small, open square are the thatched and whitewashed Drewe Arms
and the late-fifteenth-century church. The churchyard is entered
through a stone, slate-roofed lich-gate, attached to the little
sixteenth-century church house, which, like the church itself and
many of the cottages, is built of massive granite blocks from
Dartmoor.

DUNSFORD (Dv) lies along the northern slope of the Teign, north of
the road from Exeter to Moretonhampstead. Like Drewsteignton,

the village is within striking distance of Dartmoor and some of its thatched cottages are built of 'moorstone', but more of them are of cob, whitewashed or colour-washed. The church, a fourteenth- to fifteenth-century structure (except for the chancel of 1846), stands in an embanked graveyard, looking over the roofs of the houses toward the moor.

MANATON (Dv) is a delightful out-of-the-way village high up on the eastern fringe of Dartmoor, above and west of the valley of the Bovey, with lovely views of Haytor and other granite outcrops. The village of neat cottages is mostly grouped round a wedge-shaped green which is bordered by avenues of ash, oak and lime, with the fifteenth-century church close by. To the east of this is a thatched granite house, probably originally the church house.

MEVAGISSEY (Co), on a large bay to the south of St Austell, is an old fishing port that has almost grown into a town, but remains singularly unspoilt, though it is now concerned more with the holiday trade than with the fishing. The houses, built of the local slate-stone, are mostly plastered or whitewashed in the Cornish fashion and have roofs of small slates usual in the county. Mevagissey is huddled above its two harbours, the inner of which was built in the eighteenth century.

MOUSEHOLE (Co), on the west shore of Mount's Bay, south of Penzance and Newlyn, is a very attractive fishing village gathered round its small harbour, with old-world houses and engagingly narrow streets and alleys. Formerly called Port Enys, it was devastated during a Spanish raid on this part of Cornwall in 1595, when all the houses were destroyed except for the sixteenth-century manor house, part of which survives in the interesting Keigwin Arms inn.

POLPERRO (Co), perhaps the quaintest, one of the oldest, and certainly the best known of the fishing villages of south Cornwall, lies deep in a narrow ravine, between Fowey and Looe. It has exceptionally restricted streets with characteristic old houses, some of which date from the sixteenth century, winding down to its small harbour. Polperro, like Mousehole and Newlyn, has in recent years become a favourite village with artists.

PORT ISAAC (Co) is on the rugged and precipitous north coast of Cornwall, between Padstow and Boscastle, and is reached by a road down a long ridge. The secluded and old-fashioned fishing village, with steep, narrow streets, nestles round its harbour in an almost landlocked cove, dry at low tide. On either side stretches the beautiful cliff scenery for which north Cornwall is famous, and there is a view across Port Isaac Bay to Tintagel Castle on its headland.

ST BREOCK (Co), named after one of the many obscure Celtic saints, was 'Sancti Brioci de Nansent' (*i.e.* 'of the valley of the saints') in a fourteenth-century document. Hidden away in a little tributary valley of the Camel, south-west of Wadebridge, it is a delightful little village, its cottages descending the hill from the eighteenth-century manor house at the top to the low-built church, mostly of the fifteenth century, beside the stream.

ST GERMANS (Co), near the head of a long creek on the west of the Tamar, north of the Torpoint–Liskeard road, is almost a little town in character, and was in fact the cathedral city of Cornwall until 1049. The present church, consecrated in 1261, has an impressive west front with twin towers and a deeply-recessed Norman porch. The Eliot Almshouses in the village are an unusual two-storeyed group, probably of the seventeenth century, with apartments upstairs and down, the upper with balconies and overhanging gables.

VERYAN (Co), though situated high above the sea, east of the Fal estuary, is unlike most upland villages in Cornwall in that it is charmingly embosomed in trees. The church has a fourteenth-century tower built of slate, but the most distinctive feature of the village is the five round houses, whitewashed buildings with conical thatched roofs, erected according to legend to keep out the devil, but dating only from the early nineteenth century.

WIDECOMBE-IN-THE-MOOR (Dv), made famous by the song of *Widecombe Fair*, is a characteristic upland village well within the confines of Dartmoor and some distance north of the road from Ashburton to Tavistock. It lies in the valley of the Webburn, a tributary of the Dart, below the ridge which rises to the lofty Hameldown Tor, and is well grouped round its square, on one side of which soars the imposing tower, 120 feet high, of its long church, the 'Cathedral of the Moor'. Close by is the granite fifteenth-century Church House, now partly used as the village hall.

9 The Western Marches

The country of the Western Marches, between the Midland Plain and the Welsh border, shows as great a variety of scenery as can be found anywhere in England. It is a region of beautiful valleys, winding among groups of rounded hills or enclosed by long, sharp-faced escarpments, all of an immense fascination. But not only is the landscape itself stimulating, it has been less contaminated, either by industry or the modern way of life, than almost any other part of England.

The wide variety in the scenery of the marches is the result of the great complexity in the rock structure; nowhere in England, in fact, is the relationship between the landscape and the geological foundation so well displayed as here. As might be expected, where so many different strata are revealed, there is naturally a great diversity in the building materials.

In the extreme south of the borderland is the Forest of Dean, an ancient royal forest now given over to a large extent to modern afforestation, but also enclosing the only coalfield in England that has had no detrimental effect on the scenery, the collieries being mostly hidden in the dense woodlands. Of the comparatively few villages here, none is remarkable; nor are they in the enchanting ravine of the Wye, farther west, where the villager seems perhaps to have been overawed by nature. But there are good quarries of red sandstone in the Forest of Dean from which stone for the cathedrals and many of the churches of the Welsh border was produced.

The Malvern Hills, which form the scenic boundary between the lower part of the Severn Valley (included in Section 10) and the Western Marches, are made up of a granite-like gneiss and other ancient rocks, and though this is lovely country, there are no settlements here of any age. The country to the west and north-west, however, stretching past Hereford and Leominster as far as Ludlow, is of the greatest interest for the village seeker. This is the region where the Old Red Sandstone is seen to its best effect. The orchards of Herefordshire are of course famous, and there are some untilled uplands given over to sheep rearing, but the greater part of this hilly region is under the plough, and the red soil which is turned up adds attraction to the landscape, which appears even greener in comparison with the richness of the red.

The Old Red Sandstone also seems to colour all the architecture of this region. Many of the villages are built of brick, the product of the red marls found in conjunction with the sandstone, and in these villages red tiles, often of a deeper hue than the brickwork, give an added lustre to it. In other villages the red sandstone itself, which in fact varies in tone from a deep red to purple or pink or even a pinky-grey, is used to the best advantage. Unfortunately, much of the sandstone is not particularly satisfactory for building; it varies considerably in its consistency and it weathers badly, tending to split along planes parallel to the bedding of the strata. This makes it useful for walling and paving, but reduces its quality as a freestone. The older buildings of the region, however, are nearly all timber framed, and I shall return to a consideration of this in a moment.

To the north again, extending over Shropshire towards Shrewsbury, we come to a region that vies in geological complexity with west Dorset and east Somerset. Its most noticeable outcrops are the Silurian rocks, consisting principally of dark shales interbedded with limestones. The long limestone ridges which are the chief topographical feature are often wooded at the escarpment edge, though the easier dip slope is usually well cultivated, especially where the limestone sinks under the overlying shale, and in these areas villages are numerous.

The various strata yield a very marked diversity of building stones, from the yellowish rocks of the upper beds to the green of the lower layers. The rocks, especially in the neighbourhood of Church Stretton and along the boundary with the red sandstone near Ludlow, are sometimes banded with purple. Many villages around Church Stretton show the effective use made of the local sandstone with purple or yellowish-green markings. In Corve Dale and Ape Dale, under Wenlock Edge, there are small villages mostly built in the yellow-grey stone quarried from the limestone formations. All of these stones tend to be rough, especially when compared with the Cotswold limestones, and none lend themselves to decoration.

Farther west, along the border, the rocks are mostly slates and shales, more Welsh than English in character. The mention of Welsh slate brings us to the subject of roofing materials. Slates from North Wales had appeared in the Marches during the late Middle Ages, though it was not until the middle of the eighteenth century that their use became widespread here, as indeed all over England. The great advantage of the Welsh roofing slate to the builders of this time was not only that it was cheap, strong and durable, but it was thinner and lighter than any other material. A comparable roof of limestone or sandstone slabs would apparently weigh perhaps five times as much. In consequence, the walls and rafters that were to support the slate roof need be less strongly built, another advantage that commended itself. The objection today is not to the slates themselves, whether Welsh or otherwise (they look very well in their native country—the Lake District, for instance), it is to the use of dull grey uniformly-shaped slates in regions to which they are not suited. Nothing could be worse than a house with walls of rich red sandstone, of the kind to be seen in the Western Marches, and a roof of mean-looking monotonously uniform slates. (I am aware, of course, that this criticism can be made of villages in other regions, but this seems an appropriate place to give vent to it.)

In the Welsh borderland to the north of Shrewsbury, the older Silurian rocks are submerged under the Bunter and other New Red Sandstones that extend out across the Cheshire Plain and are considered in the next section.

Despite the variety of building stone to be met with in the Western Marches, it is the timberwork that has stamped its individuality on this countryside. Probably because of the great wealth of suitable trees, the border counties have always been noted for their timber building, and examples of cruck construction, which continued to be employed here until the seventeenth century, are still to be seen in humble cottages and barns. Other timber-framed buildings of all kinds—manor houses, market halls, farmsteads and cottages—ranging from the Tudor to the Georgian period, are to be seen everywhere, but especially north-west of Hereford, in the shadow of the Welsh mountains.

Here you will find a fascinating cluster of villages, built almost entirely of 'black-and-white' or 'magpie' houses, as they are sometimes called. In the cottages, wattle and daub is commonly used to fill the spaces between the black timbers, but the larger buildings frequently have an infilling of red brick or even sandstone. But whether the building be large or small, the infilling is invariably whitewashed to give it the striking black and white effect. Apart from this, the buildings show a great diversity of pattern in their decoration, and many of them are embellished with elaborate carving on their moulded beams, corner-posts, brackets, gable-end barge-boards, and the like. A variety of dormer windows, porches and balustraded balconies may also be seen. In the quantity and variety of its decoration, it may be said, if not perhaps in the quality of its building, this region of Herefordshire outstrips the wool country of East Anglia.

English rural building is not, as a rule, the outcome of prolonged study or deliberate design; it is the result of a long and slow tradition largely unaffected by outside influences and embellished only occasionally by individual fancy. Local builders must almost inevitably go unsung and even unrecorded. It is pleasant, therefore, to recall the name of John Abel, 'one of His Majesty's carpenters', who flourished at the time when timber building in the Western Marches was at its zenith. Born at Hereford, and buried at Sarnesfield in the same county in 1694 at the age of 97, he was the rare example of a craftsman who infused into the local building style a high quality of order and ornament. Though most of his work was naturally done in the towns, the old grammar school at Weobley is one of the buildings attributed to him, and his influence must have made itself felt in many other village buildings in this region.

Villages of the Western Marches

ALVELEY (Sh), west of the Kidderminster–Bridgnorth road, lies along the ridge of a hill overlooking the Severn where it breaks through the red sandstone. It has a rambling street of old cottages, mostly in sandstone and brick, and at the northern end is the restored church, from which there is a splendid view westward over the wooded banks of the river to the Clee Hills. Sandstone quarried at Alveley and Highley (on the other side of the Severn) has been used extensively in the Marches.

ATCHAM (Sh) looks well as it is approached from Shrewsbury on the Wolverhampton road, which crosses the Severn here, close to a fine eighteenth-century bridge of sandstone. Notable in the small village is the red-brick eighteenth-century inn, the Mytton and Mermaid; behind this, beside the river, is the church, of Saxon foundation. Close by are the gates of Attingham Park, a large house built in 1785 to the designs of George Steuart and now an Adult Education College, with grounds landscaped in 1797 by Humphry Repton.

BOSBURY (He), in quiet, little-known country west of the Malvern Hills, is one of the best of several villages in this hop-growing neighbourhood where black-and-white timber-framed houses predominate. The houses, of which carved barge-boards are a feature, line the south side of the street, facing the twelfth- to fifteenth-century red sandstone church, which has a curious squat detached belfry of the thirteenth century. The Crown Inn, partly of the sixteenth century, was formerly the manor house.

BREDWARDINE (He), of which Francis Kilvert, the diarist, was vicar from 1877 until his death in 1879, is a delightful village exquisitely situated in the valley of the Wye, and approached from the Hereford–Hay road by a long, quaint eighteenth-century bridge of mellow brick from which there are lovely views of the river, bordered by gardens. Near by are the Old Court, partly of the fourteenth century, the early-eighteenth-century brick Lion Inn, and the twelfth- to thirteenth-century church with its eighteenth-century tower, on a knoll above the river.

EARDISLAND (He), where the road from Leominster to Kington crosses the river Arrow, is one of the most enchanting villages in the Welsh Marches. Among its many black-and-white timber-framed houses, spaced irregularly along the road's green borders, the rambling Staick House is particularly notable; said to be of the fourteenth century, it has a remarkable roof of sandstone slates. Near the bridge over the river are the old whipping-post and sixteenth-century brick dovecot.

EARDISLEY (He), lying to the north of the Wye valley, between Hereford and Hay, belonged to one family—the Baskervilles—from the Norman Conquest until 1640. Many characteristic black-and-white timber-framed houses, some with stone roofs, are to be seen in its long street, and one of them, The Forge, shows typical cruck-framed construction of the fourteenth century. Though I have generally ignored the insides of buildings in this book, I cannot overlook the wonderful eleventh-century font in the church with its carved figures showing a survival of Celtic influence.

GARWAY (He), in a fold of the valley slopes bordering the Monnow, is little more than a hamlet, but a charming one. The fourteenth-century nave of the church—which has also a finely-carved Norman chancel—is built over the foundations of a round church of the Knights Templar. There is a detached fortress-like bell-tower of about 1200, and among the neighbouring farm buildings is an unusual vaulted and stone-roofed dovecot of the fourteenth century, with 666 nesting holes.

PEMBRIDGE (He), on the Leominster–Kington road, west of Eardisland and south of the Arrow, has many black-and-white timber-framed houses, mainly of the sixteenth and seventeenth centuries and exceptionally picturesque, but perhaps rather too crowded together. Other fine buildings include the sixteenth-century market hall, with stout timber pillars, and seventeenth-century almshouses. Close to the fourteenth-century church is a curious stone tower of the same period with a two-tiered timber belfry, looking rather like a pagoda.

WEOBLEY (He), south of the Leominster–Hay road, below the wooded Burton Hill, is perhaps the finest of the Welsh border villages. It has a great many fine timber-framed buildings showing a diversity of ornamented brackets, moulded beams, barge-boards and other work, mostly of the sixteenth and seventeenth centuries. Among the best is the seventeenth-century Grammar School, attributed to John Abel; and one cottage (formerly a large barn) still retains its original cruck construction. The large village is overlooked by the graceful seventeenth-century steeple of its church, which is otherwise of the fourteenth century.

10 The Midland Plain

The Midland Plain is a large inverted triangle whose western edge is the Welsh Marches and its south-eastern edge the limestone belt, while the Pennine Chain has driven a broad wedge into its northern side. From this central tract, thought of by many as the 'Heart of England', three long projections reach out: to the south-west (the Severn Valley, or the Vale of Gloucester, as it is sometimes called), to the north-west (the Cheshire Plain) and to the north-east (the Vale of Trent).

Let me say at once that the term 'plain' is a misnomer, for though the land within the boundaries of this triangle and its extensions is mostly of low elevation in comparison with the Pennines, the hills of the Welsh border or even the limestone uplands, it is not by any means flat. It has hills which, if they rarely rise above 500 feet and do not dominate the countryside, like the moorlands of Devon, or bound it in like the chalk hills of southern England, are made up of various kinds of rock, so that the whole area shows a greater diversity of character than is generally admitted.

Some lovers of other regions of England are scared away by the knowledge that certain areas in the northern part of the Plain have become industrialised, and they have the impression that the whole of the Midlands—at least, the North Midlands—is one vast seething hive of industry. Nothing could be farther from the truth. Industry, of course, is bound to cause some change in the character of the country in which it is situated, but the coalfields of north and south Staffordshire, north Warwickshire, Leicestershire, and Nottinghamshire and Derbyshire on which the Midland industries are based are restricted in extent, and they have had a surprisingly limited influence on the landscape—certainly when compared with the great industrial areas of Lancashire and Yorkshire—and the villages outside their boundaries have been singularly little affected. Contrasting with the industrial regions, too, are many quiet and unspoilt areas: the green meadows of the Severn and Avon valleys, the orchards of the Vale of Evesham, the oaklands of the Forest of Arden, the rich grasslands of Leicestershire and south Derbyshire, and the shady groves of Sherwood Forest, to mention only a few.

The Midland Plain was at one time covered by a thick belt of woodlands (especially of oak), which still survives to a limited extent: the names of Sherwood Forest, Cannock Chase and the Forest of Arden are reminders of this. The woodlands were cleared for cultivation only slowly, after the lighter soil of the Cotswolds and other limestone uplands had already been brought under the plough. As the colonisation went forward, many small villages were established at irregular intervals in the Plain. They are mostly much closer together than those of the Cotswolds, and the large nucleated village which developed elsewhere is less frequently met with in the Midlands. The nature of the colonisation, too, meant that villages, instead of being grouped round a central green or square, tend to straggle out along several roads diverging from a particular point.

The heavy soils of the Midland Plain are the product of the clays and marls that extend throughout this region. These deposits are of two distinct types and the boundary between them is marked approximately by the Severn and the lower part of its tributary, the Warwickshire Avon, continued beyond Stratford by the line of the ancient Fosse Way, which ran north-east to Leicester and thence to Lincoln. The clay to the east of this line, stretching to the foot of the limestone escarpment, is that of the Lower Lias formation, the lower member of a series of strata another of which (the Middle Lias) we met in the limestone country. The Lower Lias consists mainly of a stiff pale blue or grey-blue deposit (hence its other name, the Blue Lias); the blueness is caused by the presence of a limestone which is the source of important lime and cement works. The gently undulating country, its monotony relieved by its being pushed up into ridges here and there, is largely given over to pasture; the attractive villages, invariably small, are mostly built of brick, though ironstone takes the place of this near the limestone escarpment. (The geological map of Britain, incidentally, confuses the layman by showing the Lower and Middle Lias in the same colour, so it is impossible to tell from the map where the boundary lies. The two strata, as I have said, are quite distinct in their make up and in their influence on the landscape.)

To the west of the line from the lower Avon to the Fosse Way, the deposits belong to the New Red Sandstone group. The most important of them is a broad band of Keuper Sandstones (pronounced 'koi-per'), the name given to a combination of soft red clays and calcareous marls which when newly ploughed give a pleasant warmth to the landscape. In the great tract of these extending over the upper Avon valley to the vales of Worcestershire, the Midland Plain is seen at its best. This is the England associated with Shakespeare, its lanes bordered by great oaks and other trees, its fields fringed with hedges that seem greener by comparison with the ploughed red fields, and its numerous villages notable for their brick and thatched timber-framed cottages, with flowery gardens fronting the lanes.

The Keuper sandstones extend down the western side of the Severn valley and are among the red formations rising to the shoulders of the Malvern Hills. The lias and red sandstone deposits on either side of the

34 *Weobley, Herefordshire*

Severn in the Vale of Gloucester underlie a broad expanse of fertile meadowland, where villages are gathered more thickly than in the central part of the Plain. In the other direction, the Keuper sandstones stretch north-east from Leicester and Nottingham down the Vale of Trent towards the Humber. The Trent runs through a band of the red marls, but the villages in this district are nowhere near as attractive as those in the Vale of Severn, either in their setting or their building.

The Keuper sandstones are intercepted by older outcrops that make for diversity in the Midland Plain. In Charnwood Forest, north-west of Leicester, an intrusion of the oldest rocks in England comes through to the surface. This rugged little piece of country was once even better wooded than it is now and there are no ancient settlements here. Running north and south to the west of Coventry is a broad belt of Permian Sandstone, forming a tract of pleasantly undulating country that extends as far as Kenilworth. The distinctive deep red sandstone is perhaps best seen in the ruins of the great castle, but the stone has been used also in the churches and houses of many small villages in this neighbourhood.

The other of the two important deposits of the New Red Sandstone occurring in the Midlands is the Bunter Sandstone. This consists of a series of hard gravelly beds, showing as strips running north and south on either side of the coal measures of the Black Country. The strata mostly come to the surface as low rolling country and their dry, sandy soils were among the last to be brought under cultivation. Extensive tracts of natural heathland still survive and are well seen in Cannock Chase and in Sutton Park near Birmingham. The Bunter sandstones are also responsible for the precipitous crag on which Nottingham Castle stands and from which they stretch northward through Sherwood Forest. As might be expected from what I have said of the soil, ancient settlements on these sandstones are comparatively few.

In the Black Country and the north Staffordshire coalfield, the New Red Sandstone is interspersed with areas of clay mixed with shale, resulting in the dull grey soil that seems inevitably to be found with the Coal Measures. The villages here are consequently poor, even apart from their contamination by the coal workings. Plain brick is the unfailing building material, and the villages built of dull brick, or extended by dull streets in this material during their conversion into

35 *Wilmcote, Warwickshire: Mary Arden's House*

colliery communities, are the architectural price paid for the Industrial Revolution.

The Cheshire Plain, which extends north-west from this region towards the Welsh border, consists basically of a huge expanse of red Keuper marls mostly bordered by outcrops of Bunter and other sandstones. This again is quietly undulating country rather than a plain; it has many streams flowing in wide valleys, with a pleasing pattern of red and green in the fields and hedgerows. The characteristic red sandstone and black-and-white timber-framed buildings of Cheshire can be seen also on the other side of the Mersey, in Lancashire, though precious few of the villages here have survived from the demands made by the Industrial Revolution.

Not only in the Cheshire Plain but all over the west Midlands, the warm-hued New Red Sandstones are the chief building material. Their rough texture and their colour, which varies through a wide range of reds, make them attractive, but most of the red sandstones show all too clearly the effects of weathering, though there are some good quality stones (pink stone from Hollington, near Uttoxeter, was chosen for Coventry cathedral). Sandstone has gone into many churches in the western part of the region, but elsewhere in the Midlands where there was a lack of adequate building stone, the church builder brought his stone from a neighbouring region: from the Cotswolds for the churches in the south, from the limestone quarries at Ancaster in Lincolnshire for many churches in the east Midlands. But the village builder found it too expensive to quarry and transport stone for his smaller and humbler dwellings. It was cheaper to draw on the abundant supplies of timber from the forests, while these lasted, and later to make bricks from the local clays.

Red brick and black timber, then, are the principal materials used in village building over much of the Midland Plain. The older buildings seem invariably to have been of typical cruck construction, and though there are not so many survivals as in the Welsh Marches, cruck-framed buildings are still to be seen, especially in Leicestershire and Cheshire. All the timber-framed buildings had originally an infilling of mud or plaster, but later brick began to take the place of these. In either case, as in the Welsh Marches, the infilling was invariably whitewashed (lime-washed, to be precise) and it is this famous black-and-white effect that is the most characteristic feature of the villages in the Midland Plain; it ranges from the Western Marches to the Vale of Trent. In the west Midlands the larger buildings are richly and often fancifully decorated. Regional features are the fitting of a shaped coving below the overhang of the upper storeys and of eaves with timbers shaped to the cove below the roof. The liking for timber-framing, too, sometimes extends to the churches. Unfortunately, some buildings which appear to be timber-framed are seen at close quarters to be entirely of brick, blackened and whitened to simulate the impression of timber-framing. (This reprehensible practice is not confined to the Midlands by any means, though it seems to be rather more prevalent here.)

Brick had been known in the Midlands since the fifteenth century, but it was not employed on any large scale until the supplies of good timber began to run low. The variety of clays has resulted in a considerable variety of colouring in the brickwork. Some of the bricks tend to be rather strident in their effects; they fit best into the rich green landscapes of the west Midlands. Many brick houses of the eighteenth century have survived, but Victorian brickwork has unhappily played havoc in many Midland villages and there are few that remain anything like intact from the best period of English rural building.

Though tiles are to be seen in plenty in the Midland Plain, thatch was formerly the characteristic roof covering. Tiles had, however, been produced in the Midlands since the fifteenth and sixteenth centuries, and by the middle of the nineteenth century, Staffordshire and Shropshire formed the most important tile-making region in England. On the other side of the region, pantiles are familiar in parts of Leicestershire and Nottinghamshire; no doubt they were originally brought up the Trent from Holland. Despite the presence of sandstone over much of the region, stone slate roofs are less common than in the Western Marches. A local speciality was the slate quarried around the edge of Charnwood Forest (usually called Swithland slate); this was in great demand for roofing in the east Midlands at the end of the eighteenth century, before the cheaper Welsh slates began to flood the market.

Villages of the Midland Plain

(a) The West Midlands:

BIDFORD-ON-AVON (Wa) is on the Stratford–Evesham road, in the pleasant vale of the Avon. It is attractively situated on the north side of the river, here crossed by a fine fifteenth-century bridge, and has several old houses, chiefly of brick, but including the former Falcon Inn, a stone building mostly of the sixteenth century. This stands to the north of the large church, whose thirteenth- to fourteenth-century tower rises among the trees on the high bank of the river.

BRETFORTON (Wo) is a peaceful and unspoilt village in the Vale of Evesham, east of that delightful town. Its old timber-framed inn, the Fleece, painted by Sargent, has a roof of Cotswold slates and is always gay with flowers. Many of the houses date from the sixteenth century, when the village was sold to the tenants. It previously belonged to the abbey of Evesham, of whose grange there remains a fifteenth-century tithe-barn, the fish-pond and a dovecot; in all there are six dovecots in the village, one with 800 nesting holes and another turned into a cottage.

CHADDESLEY CORBETT (Wo) lies off the Bromsgrove–Kidderminster road, to the north of which rise the Clent Hills and is enclosed by great trees. Though small, it is an architectural delight, with a rich assortment of red-brick houses, some of them dating from the eighteenth century, and others with black-and-white timber-framing, including the Talbot Inn—all dominated by the lofty eighteenth-century spire of the church, which is of red sandstone and has excellent work of the twelfth and fourteenth centuries.

CLEEVE PRIOR (Wo), on the east side of the Avon downstream from Bidford, is an exceptionally flowery village, its dignified stone houses with thatched and red-tiled roofs set back behind broad green verges. The long street ends at a triangular green, and off this is placed the twelfth- to fourteenth-century church, which has a fine fifteenth-century tower with unusual decoration. In the churchyard is a yew perhaps 600 years old, and there are clipped yews round the old manor house with its tall chimneys.

DUNCHURCH (Wa) is a pleasant ridge-top village on the Daventry–Coventry road (now fortunately left quieter by the M 1 extension).

Opposite the Dun Cow, an eighteenth-century coaching inn, are the steps of the old market cross, and in the little market place are the village stocks. To the east is a timber-framed house with an overhanging upper storey, probably of the fifteenth century, formerly the Lion Inn and a meeting-place of the Gunpowder Plot conspirators. The fourteenth-century church near by is built of the local red sandstone.

ELMLEY CASTLE (Wo), on the northern slopes of the prominent Bredon Hill (an outlier of the limestone), is perhaps the most enchanting of the Midland villages. The church has work of every period from the eleventh to the sixteenth century, and the exquisite little square is set round with an engaging medley of houses of various periods, some showing timber-framing (including the charming black-and-white Queen Elizabeth Inn) and some of brick and stone, all backed by the delightfully wooded hill slopes.

FRAMPTON-ON-SEVERN (Gl) is near the broadening of the river into its estuary, at the south end of the Vale of Gloucester, faced by the Cotswold Hills on one side and the heights of the Forest of Dean on the other. Beautifully approached from the Gloucester–Bristol road, it is a charming village, with many lovely cottages, some of brick, some timber-framed, most of them with thatched roofs, scattered around a long, wide green.

LITTLE COMBERTON (Wo) is a tranquil village with lovely old timber-framed cottages, thatched or tiled, north of Bredon Hill and south of the Evesham–Pershore road. In the yard of a fine black-and-white timbered farmhouse is a round stone dovecot with nearly 700 nesting holes, and there is another dovecot in the grounds of the manor house. The church has a fourteenth-century tower and a seventeenth-century porch with an older oak arch and a Norman doorway. Other delightful thatched and timber-framed houses can be seen at GREAT COMBERTON, to the south-west, near the Avon.

MERIDEN (Wa) is an attractive but somewhat straggling village with a variety of eighteenth-century houses on the Coventry–Birmingham road, now fortunately avoided by the new motorway. On the green near the west end is the medieval cross, which by a Warwickshire tradition marks the very centre of England, and farther west is Forest Hall, built by Joseph Bonomi in 1788 and still the headquarters of the Woodmen of Arden, an archery society known to have been in existence before 1785.

OFFENHAM (Wo), on the east bank of the Avon above Evesham, lies among orchards and has an early-fifteenth-century church tower, facing across the river, and a wide street which displays a mingling of stone and timber-framed houses, with many low thatched eaves. Near the end is the Bridge Inn, from which gardens slope down to the ferry connecting Offenham with NORTON, on the Evesham–Alcester road, another village with many timber-framed houses, and also a fourteenth- to fifteenth-century church.

PRESTON-ON-STOUR (Wa) is a well-kept brick-built village on the west bank of the river, in the quiet pastoral country south of Stratford-on-Avon and reached from the Oxford road. A row of nineteenth-century model cottages leads to the green, with the church above (much altered in 1757), standing in an embanked churchyard and approached through fine eighteenth-century ironwork gates and a tunnel of yews.

PRIORS MARSTON (Wa) is on the slopes of a hill, north of the limestone country, and south-east of Southam by the Welsh road, an old drover's route through the Midlands. Among its many attractive houses is the seventeenth-century Falcon Inn, with mullioned windows, and the Vicarage, built in the seventeenth century as a farmhouse, but enlarged in the eighteenth. A village chair-making industry has been established, and hand-made bricks are produced at Marston Hill.

STONELEIGH (Wa), a very attractive village on the Sowe, just above the point where this river joins the Avon, has many delightful stone and brick-and-timber cottages, some of which line a green. The church, on the south side of the village, is partly of the twelfth century; north-west of it is the fine timber-framed sixteenth- to seventeenth-century manor house. The Coventry–Leamington road, crossing the Sowe, skirts the park of Stoneleigh Abbey, now the permanent show-ground of the Royal Agricultural Society.

TREDINGTON (Wa) is in the pleasant Stour valley and mostly scattered about a large irregularly-shaped green, just off the busy road between Stratford and Oxford. The village in its building is almost an outpost of the limestone country which the valley penetrates farther south. It has a variety of attractive old houses and barns, and a twelfth- to fifteenth-century church with a distinctive fourteenth-century tower and tall spire.

WELFORD-ON-AVON (Wa), one of the most charming villages in the Avon valley, lies in a wide bend of the river south of the Stratford–Evesham road, with numerous charming cottages enclosed by orchards. The striped maypole on the green is only the most recent of a succession that have stood here over the centuries. The churchyard, farther west, is surrounded by a pretty group of thatched cottages and entered through a lich-gate with fifteenth-century timbers.

(b) *The North Midlands*:

BLYTH (Nt), in a bend of the little river Ryton, a tributary of the Trent, is situated where the Ollerton–Bawtry road crosses that from East Retford to Rotherham. It is a dignified village of brick, with some colour-wash, its central green commanded by the church, which incorporates the bold early-Norman nave of a Benedictine priory church. Other notable buildings include the Spital Almshouses at the south end of the wide main street, and there is an eighteenth-century bridge over the river.

BOTTESFORD (Le), in the Vale of Belvoir, on the Nottingham–Grantham road, is a characteristic north Midland village which has a beautiful and interesting late-fourteenth-century church with a soaring crocketed spire. To the south of the churchyard is the narrow and picturesque Fleming's Bridge, built about 1500, and to the north are the Duke's Almshouses, founded in 1612. The village still retains its old cross, as well as its stocks and whipping-post.

BREEDON-ON-THE-HILL (Le), on the road from Nottingham to Birmingham, lies at the foot of a curiously isolated limestone knoll which is capped by its church, seen from many places far away across the Trent. The church, consisting of the thirteenth-century chancel and the tower of an Augustinian priory founded before 1122, is especially remarkable for a sculptured frieze assigned to the late eighth century and surviving from a Saxon monastery established here. On the green of the attractive village is an unusual stone circular war memorial.

HODNET (Sh), on the way from Shrewsbury to Market Drayton and in the Cheshire Plain, is a roadside village with attractive houses, many of them timber-framed, others of red brick. The red sand-stone church, which has an octagonal tower and an unusual gabled east end, occupies a strategic position on a rise. The early nineteenth-century parsonage, in the Tudor style, was built by Bishop Heber when rector here. At Home Farm there is a mag-nificent tithe-barn dated 1619, its timber framework mostly filled with brick nogging.

LINBY (Nt), north of Hucknall and just outside the Nottinghamshire coalfield, is a pleasant village with stone cottages on either side of the stream running along the broad main street. It has two crosses: one medieval (though restored) with a seven-sided base; the other of the seventeenth century. The churchyard contains the graves of over 150 children who died while working in the Castle Mill, east of the village, where James Watt installed in 1785 the first steam-engine used for cotton spinning—two reflections on village industry.

PRESTBURY (Ch) lies to the west of the Macclesfield–Manchester road, in pleasant undulating country typical of the Cheshire Plain, but within sight of the Peakland hills. In the graveyard of the thirteenth-to fifteenth-century church is a beautiful Norman chapel and opposite is a charming fifteenth-century priest's house, character-istically of black-and-white timber-framing. There are other attractive houses in this well-known village, which is fast becoming a favoured residential centre for commuters from Manchester.

REPTON (Db), famous for its public school, founded in 1557, and its partly-Saxon church, is on the south side of the Trent and reached from the Derby–Burton road. It was the capital of the Saxon kingdom of Mercia and the seat of a bishop, and its church, marked by a slender spire, has a tenth-century chancel with a remarkable crypt of the seventh century below. The school buildings, entered through the fourteenth-century gateway of an Augustinian priory which stood here, seem an integral part of the village, which is centred round its restored medieval cross.

STYAL (Ch), in the Bollin Valley between Wilmslow and Ringway Airport, and now only just beyond the fringe of Manchester, is a remarkably complete survival of a late-eighteenth-century in-dustrial village, built to support the Quarry Bank Cotton Mill, opened in 1784. The village, with a long reach of the pleasant

36 *Bonsall, Derbyshire*

valley that includes a timber-framed farmhouse, is now in the safe keeping of the National Trust.

SUDBURY (Db) is an exquisite small village consisting of a single street of seventeenth-century brick cottages, with the delightful Vernon Arms of 1671 among them, on the road from Derby to Uttoxeter. Beyond the west end of the street, and well seen from the road, is the striking red-brick mansion of Sudbury Hall, begun in 1613 and enlarged by George Vernon between 1670 and 1695. Its charming gardens reach down to a wood-fringed lake.

TONG (Sh), some distance north-west of Wolverhampton on the road to Chester, has a fine early-fifteenth-century church that has been called a miniature Westminster Abbey on account of its array of monuments. East of the church are many interesting houses, including the timber-framed Church Farm and a group of eighteenth-century brick houses consisting of the Post Office, the Red House, the almshouses, built round three sides of a quadrangle, and finally the Vicarage.

11 The Pennines

The Pennine Chain, the backbone of northern England, extending from the Peak District to the hills of the Scottish Border, is a range of high moorlands and fells, measuring some 140 miles from the Weaver Hills at the southern end to the South Tyne gap which separates the Pennines from the Border hills. This would be a long, formidable barrier were it not deeply indented by many dales, and also broken in several places, such as the Aire Gap between Keighley in Yorkshire and Clitheroe in Lancashire, and the less pronounced Stainmore Gap between Barnard Castle in County Durham and Appleby in Westmorland.

Geologically, the Pennines consist of immensely thick beds of Carboniferous Limestone and the overlying Millstone Grit, uplifted in an anticlinal fold, that is, in the form of an arch. Over much of the area, however, the Millstone Grit has been worn through, exposing a vast expanse of the Limestone. Considering only their surface rocks, the Pennines can be divided into three sections: first, a belt of Carboniferous Limestone stretching from Dovedale and the Weavers to the Hope Valley; then a belt of Millstone Grit extending approximately to the

Calder Valley of Lancashire and to Skipton and round Nidderdale; and finally a much larger section of the Limestone reaching to the Border, and spreading out over north Lancashire and round the Lake District on the one hand and over the greater part of Northumberland on the other. On either side of the range, as far north as Bradford and Burnley, are the Coal Measures on which the industrial wealth of Yorkshire and Lancashire depends.

For the purpose of this survey, I have cut the Pennines at the Stainmore Gap, south of the Tees, and dealt only with the Peak District and that part of the main chain which includes the Yorkshire Dales. It may seem illogical thus to divide the northern section of the Carboniferous Limestone, but in fact the fells and moors of Durham and Northumberland bear only a superficial resemblance to those of Yorkshire and Derbyshire; they have much more in common with the coastal regions of the two north-east counties, certainly as far as the villages are concerned.

The Carboniferous Limestone is so called because it is part of a geological group that includes the Coal Measures, and it is often found in association with outcrops of these; but a more realistic name, I think, is the alternative Mountain Limestone, and this is the one I shall use from here on. The Mountain Limestone, unlike the chalk and the oolitic limestone, shows no continuous outcrop extending right across England. It was laid down at a much earlier stage than these other rocks, and consequently it appears only where the many overlying deposits have been eroded or where subsequent folding of the strata has brought it to the surface. As a result of one or other of these occurrences, it does outcrop in many parts of Britain; we have seen it already in the Mendip Hills and the Forest of Dean, and it appears also in Wales in the Gower peninsula and Pembrokeshire and the Great Orme near Llandudno, as well as in the Isle of Man and Scotland.

In the two sections we are concerned with here, the southern part of the Peak District (sometimes called the 'Low Peak') and the Yorkshire fells, the limestone country is easily recognisable by the pale grey or blue-grey of the stone, which turns to a dazzling white when the sun brings out the colour, and by the smoothly undulating uplands, almost devoid of trees and divided by characteristic dry-stone walls (*i.e.* built without mortar) into a white-bound chequerwork of rich green fields. This upland plateau, great areas of which reach well over 1,000 feet, is dissected by many deep and narrow ravines, often charmingly wooded, whose sides are bare gleaming crags of the limestone.

On these limestone uplands, the farms are scattered and they are chiefly concerned with sheep grazing, but the stone-built villages are not confined to the valleys. Indeed some of the dales are too restricted to hold a village of any size. The Mountain Limestone differs considerably in its structure from the oolitic limestone of the Cotswolds, and the villages, understandably, differ too. The exposed rocks of the Mountain Limestone appear as thick, massive beds; they are harder and rougher than the oolitic limestones and because of this the stone does not lend itself so freely to ornament or to such elegance of building as we find in the Cotswolds. The limestone houses in the Peak are simpler and more solid.

As I mentioned, the Mountain Limestone has been shaped by primeval forces into an arch or anticline, and it dips to the east and west under the moorlands of the Millstone Grit. Between the limestone and the gritstone there are beds of much softer shales (sometimes called the Yoredale Beds) and these have been utilised by the rivers, the Derwent in its beautiful valley on the east and the equally lovely Dove and Manifold for some distance on the west. (A geological curiosity is that both the Derwent and the Dove leave the shales for a time to push their way through tortuous ravines in the limestone: the former between Matlock and Cromford, and the latter through the famous gorge of Dovedale.)

The Millstone (or Moorstone) Grit which makes up the High Peak and the barren moorlands stretching north towards Wharfedale is responsible for some of the highest and wildest country in England, reaching over 2,000 feet in places. This is a bleak and desolate region, covered with heather and split up by numerous peat bogs; its character is well seen in the heights of Kinder Scout and Bleaklow and the moors extolled by the Brontës. Though surrounded by the highest density of population in England—such teeming cities as Manchester, Sheffield and Bradford are within a few miles—this region is among the most sparsely inhabited in the country. The moorland plateaux, however, are intersected by deep valleys, invariably cultivated except where they are given over to industry (as in the woollen districts of Yorkshire), and the tops of the valleys are lined by scarps of hard dark crag called 'edges'.

The Millstone Grit is in fact a rough, tough, pebbly gritstone of a very coarse texture. Sometimes mistaken for granite (as Charlotte Brontë did in *Jane Eyre*), it has been suggested that the gritstone may have been produced by the denudation of some great granitic mass. Sheep are maintained on the moors, but for mile after mile the only signs of the handiwork of man are the dark gritstone walls, and the only habitations are the remote dark grey farms. The stone cannot bring brightness to the landscape, as it does in the limestone districts. The villages avoid the moorlands and are all to be found down in the dales, or at least below the limits of cultivation at the edge of the moors.

Though it is a hard, coarse stone, difficult to work, the Millstone Grit has been used for building since early times; its imperviousness was no doubt in its favour. Castles, churches and bridges were built of it, as well as the simple, unadorned houses, and it was transported to the East Riding and Lincolnshire for church building, even in Saxon times. Timber had never been used to any large extent in the Pennines and their surroundings, and after it became scarce, towards the end of the Tudor period, houses were almost all built of gritstone. Thinly-bedded varieties of the gritstone were used as flagstones and often as roofing slabs.

The paucity of cultivable land in the moorland region naturally long restricted the population of the dales. But in the seventeenth century there came a great development in the woollen industry, and the expansion of home weaving led to the building of stone cottages with long windows giving more light to the single room upstairs where the weaving was done. These weavers' houses, quite a number of which survive, are a feature confined to the gritstone country of Yorkshire and Lancashire. They mostly range in date from the seventeenth to the early nineteenth century, and are gathered together in many places around Huddersfield, Penistone, Oldham and Rochdale, but a special-ised study of such early industrial communities has yet to be made. Their counterparts are the manor houses of the wealthier cloth merchants that are a speciality of the Halifax and Huddersfield district.

A woollen industry had existed in the West Riding since at least as early as the fourteenth century, though at first it was merely a supplement to sheep raising. By the Tudor period it had grown in importance, if less so than in other parts of the country like the Cotswolds and East Anglia. The introduction of water power led to a further development of industry in villages which could make use of the rapid streams in the valleys. But the greatest expansion came with the introduction of steam power and its concomitant, the factory system. The presence of the Coal Measures on the east of the Pennines helped to centralise the industry here to the exclusion of manufacturing districts farther away from the new source of power. The villages grew rapidly into towns (and the towns into larger towns), though among their great expanse of new building they frequently preserved some semblance of their former character.

In association with the Coal Measures there are grey shales suitable for brick-making, alternating with bands of grey or buff-coloured sandstones, which are invariably to be seen in the older buildings. Sandstone quarried in the neighbourhood of Leeds, Bradford and Halifax, and commonly known as York Stone, was used extensively in the industrial districts; it is hard, strong and durable, but is not suitable for roofing as it tends to hold the moisture, and the sandstone slates were more often brought from the Millstone Grit areas ('thack-stones', as they are called locally, were used in the Colne valley above Huddersfield as early as the thirteenth century). But these stone slabs have been superseded in many villages by the inevitable Welsh slate.

The Millstone Grit has outliers in the Forest of Rossendale (sand-stone roofing slates from this area could once be seen over much of Lancashire) and in the moors between Bolton and Blackburn, as well as in the Forest of Bowland, where the West Riding pushes out towards the Lancashire coast. But from Skipton and the middle of Wharfedale northward, except for isolated patches, as in the moors around the head of Swaledale, the landscape is dominated by the Mountain Limestone.

The most distinctive feature of this region is the great fracture known as the Craven Fault, resulting in a long crag-like escarpment which runs across the Pennines from upper Lonsdale eastward to Settle and across Wharfedale to Nidderdale. To the south of the Fault, where the limestone has disappeared deep under the gound, the upper strata are composed of shales, softer and more easily eroded. In consequence, the surface has been worn down and the landscape has become more subdued in character, though relieved by numerous knolls of unknown origin. Grey limestones and the fine-grained buff sandstones are employed for almost all the building in this area.

The vast empty country to the north of the Craven Fault is an immense sheep-run, divided by limestone walls, as in the Peak, and enlivened by great crags and scars and rock pavements. Farther north, the limestone is intermixed with various shales and sandstones, or capped by surviving outliers of the gritstone, and from Swaledale to Ribblesdale the villages are mostly built with these rough gritstones and sandstones, though the houses are frequently whitewashed. The growth of the villages in Swaledale, one of the deepest and wildest of the dales, was influenced by lead mining, an industry which was started by the Romans and which flourished for centuries.

The limestone country of West Yorkshire bears only a general resemblance to that of the Peak District; the dales, though likewise famous for their beauty, are longer and broader, and mostly given over to pasture. These dales are traversed by fast-flowing rivers, and the sites of many of the villages have been determined by the positions of ancient bridges placed where the rivers could be crossed. The villages of the Yorkshire Dales are among the most satisfying in England. Appropriately built of the Pennine stones, they have a natural dignity which is in accord with the natural beauty of their situation. The contrast between such villages, seeming to grow out of the fells, and the uniform dull brick rows of mean dwellings in the colliery villages of the Victorian era or the ill-adapted materials and styles of most of the residential expansions of our towns and cities, not only in the West Riding, of course, but all over the country, is a painful reflection on modern civilisation.

Villages of the Pennines

(a) *South of the Aire Gap:*

ALTON (St) is romantically situated on steep slopes above the narrow valley of the Churnet (a tributary of the Dove), south of the Weaver Hills, the 'last of the Pennines'. Perched on a high sandstone cliff are the ruins of a twelfth-century castle, in the grounds of a Rhenish-looking convent building of the nineteenth century by the elder Pugin, while the beautiful and very popular gardens of Alton Towers face the village across the deep and rugged glen.

BRADFIELD (YWR) is delightfully situated on the steep slopes above the valley of the river Loxley, on the edge of the wild moors that stretch away to the Derbyshire border. The chief street, which has a dignified row of stone cottages, is built along the hillside, with a large and handsome church, mostly of the fifteenth century, at the end. It is difficult to realise that this remote and secluded village is only a few miles from the smoke and grime of Sheffield.

CASTLETON (Db), finely situated in an almost enclosed dale between the limestone and the gritstone country, is a good centre for the rugged country of the High Peak. On a precipitous crag above the village is the twelfth-century keep and part of the original outer wall of Peveril Castle, founded by William Peveril, a favourite of the Conqueror, in 1068. Castleton is also famous for its underground caverns, the gaping entrance to the nearest of which, Peak Cavern, is just outside the village and right under Peveril Castle.

CROMFORD (Db) is at the south end of the dramatic limestone gorge through which the Derwent forces itself below Matlock. In the wide main street, opening on the west, is the Greyhound Inn, a fine building of the mid-eighteenth century, and in the road leading to the fifteenth-century bridge (which has some remains of a contemporary chapel attached to it) is the cotton-spinning mill established by Sir Richard Arkwright in 1771, the first in England to be operated by water power (now a colour factory). Willersley Castle, on the other side of the Derwent, was built for Arkwright in 1788.

DELPH and DOBCROSS (YWR), respectively north and south of the Oldham–Huddersfield road, near the head of the Tame valley and below the bleak Saddleworth moors, were important centres of clothmaking in the eighteenth century and still retain their old cobbled streets and stone weavers' houses. These are remarkable for their wide, low windows, mostly on the upper floor only.

DOWNHAM (La) lies east of the Clitheroe–Skipton road, in a quiet little side valley some distance above the Ribble, and at the northern foot of the prominent Pendle Hill. It is an exceptionally pretty village of stone houses, mostly of the seventeenth century, embosomed among trees, its single street running up past the sixteenth-century manor house (remodelled in 1835), the village stocks and the green to the fifteenth-century tower of the church on the crest of the rise.

EYAM (Db) is an interesting Peakland village well situated below an edge of the moorlands, west of and high above the Derwent valley. Outside the thirteenth- to fifteenth-century church is a fine Saxon cross, and round the churchyard are several pleasant eighteenth-century houses and cottages, in one of which the terrible plague that devastated the village in 1665-6 is said to have started. Farther west is the gabled Eyam Hall, a pleasing stone manor house of 1676, and opposite this are the old stocks.

HAWORTH (YWR) is famous for its associations with the Brontës, whose home was at the parsonage, built about 1800 and still maintained as far as possible as it was in their day. Standing high on the steep slopes above a tributary of the Aire which debouches at Keighley, Haworth is a characteristic stone-built village on the edge of the windswept moors made famous by *Wuthering Heights* and *Jane Eyre*. The church, rebuilt in 1881 except for the tower, contains the graves of Charlotte and Emily; the old Black Bull Inn below was the haunt of the unhappy Branwell Brontë.

HEPTONSTALL (YWR), precariously perched on a ridge between two narrow wooded glens and reached from the Calder valley at Hebden Bridge by a precipitous ascent, is an exceptionally interesting village, with houses of the dark gritstone. The old-fashioned weavers' houses with their long, mullioned windows can be seen here to perfection. The picturesque ruins of the thirteenth-century church, to which a fortress-like tower was added in the fifteenth century, still stand in the churchyard of the imposing new church of 1854.

ILAM (St) is more remarkable for its setting that for the architecture of the village itself, which consists mainly of a group of model cottages of the nineteenth century. It is splendidly situated where the Manifold emerges from a lovely wooded glen, a little before joining the Dove, which itself has forced its way through the incomparable Dovedale. The village stands at the gates of Ilam Hall, a nineteenth-century Gothic mansion (now a youth hostel), and its churchyard contains two Saxon crosses.

TIDESWELL (Db) is in the open limestone country of the Peak District, between the Chesterfield–Manchester road and the valley of the

Wye at Millers Dale. It lies in a sheltered hollow and all that can be seen from the surrounding uplands is the magnificent tower of the large and beautiful fourteenth-century church, the 'cathedral of the Peak'. Tideswell is an old-world village with houses built of the local grey limestone: the Grammar School near the church was founded in 1559; the George Hotel in the square, farther down, dates from the eighteenth century.

TISSINGTON (Db) is famous for its colourful custom of 'well-dressing' with pictures made of flower-petal mosaic, celebrated on Ascension Day. The delectable village has many eighteenth-century and other cottages in the neighbourhood of its pond and the long green stretching up between the church, which is mostly Norman, with a broad tower, and Tissington Hall, which stands in the centre of the village, not aloof from it. The hall, an early-seventeenth-century stone house enlarged at various times, has a pleasant walled garden.

WINSTER (Db), on the steep hillside above a wooded tributary valley of the Derwent, north-west of Matlock, is an enchantingly old-fashioned village, with cottages climbing the slopes rather in the manner of a Cornish fishing village. Along the main street are excellent eighteenth-century stone houses that recall Winster's former prosperity as a centre of lead-mining, and in the centre is the picturesque Market House, of the late seventeenth or early eighteenth century.

(b) *North of the Aire Gap*:

BAINBRIDGE (YNR), a very pleasant village with a spacious green, lies in an open position in the lovely pastoral Wensleydale, at the base of the flat-topped hill of Addleborough. Bainbridge was on the edge of the old forest of Wensleydale, and the custom is still maintained of sounding a horn every winter's night (at 9 o'clock) to guide belated travellers on the fells. On the green are the remains of the old stocks, and at the edge is the Rose and Crown Inn, dating from the fifteenth century.

BURNSALL (YWR) is on a beautiful reach of the Wharfe, about half-way along the length of the green, pastoral dale, in the limestone district of Craven that has so many enchanting villages. Near the sixteenth-century church (which is in a style characteristic of Craven) is a charming early-seventeenth-century Grammar School, with a gabled porch and mullioned windows, looking more like the manor house than a school. The churchyard is entered by a fine lich-gate, perhaps of the seventeenth century.

CASTLE BOLTON (YNR), on the northern slopes of Wensleydale, is more completely dominated even than Dunster or Bamburgh by its great feudal castle. The wide grass-bordered street with its humble grey stone cottages contrasts effectively with the gaunt but well-preserved late-fourteenth-century stronghold of the noble family of Scrope, who were Wardens of the Western Marches for over 250 years. The towering castle occupies a commanding position looking out over the whole wide middle reach of the dale.

DENT (YWR), on the west side of the Pennines in the remote and beautiful Dentdale, whose river runs down to join the Lune below Sedbergh, is an unusually quaint village with a narrow and tortuous cobbled street round which the houses of grey stone, some of them colour-washed, are huddled in a picturesque manner. The green pastures gathered round the village contrast vividly with the houses and contrast, too, with the wild fells above. Dent was famous until the beginning of the nineteenth century for its knitted worsted stockings.

GIGGLESWICK (YWR), on the opposite side of the Ribble from Settle, is an old-fashioned village entrancingly situated at the foot of Giggleswick Scar, part of the long Craven Fault. It retains its old market cross and stocks, and has several good houses of the seventeenth and eighteenth centuries, some with their door lintels decorated in the typical Craven fashion. The buildings, mostly Victorian, of the public school founded in 1512 are grouped together on the west side of the village.

GRASSINGTON (YWR), an exceptionally picturesque village that is almost a little town in character, is on the east side of a broad reach of Wharfedale, between Burnsall and Kettlewell. Its narrow cobbled street, with characteristic grey houses, leads steeply up to the little square with the town hall at the top. Grassington Hall, on the main road at the foot of the hill, incorporates part of a late-thirteenth-century house, with Tudor and nineteenth-century additions. The bridge over the river below the rocky channel of Ghaistrill's Strid is basically medieval.

HAREWOOD (YWR), delightfully positioned on a ridge south of the Wharfe, on the road between Leeds and Harrogate, is a dignified village of stone-built terraces. These were designed by John Carr of York in 1760 for Edwin Lascelles, an ancestor of the Princess Royal and her son, the Earl of Harewood, who live at Harewood House, a stately mansion built by Carr and Robert Adam in 1759–71. The main street of the village leads to the gates of the park, which was laid out by 'Capability' Brown and contains the fifteenth-century parish church.

KETTLEWELL (YWR) is a secluded village with many characteristic stone houses, some of them whitewashed, in the centre of the limestone district of Craven. It lies among trees along both sides of the Park Gill Beck, which has scrieved a deep cleft in the dale side on its way to reach the open, green pastures of Wharfedale. Kettlewell was a market town in the Middle Ages, and the manorial rights are still kept in trust and the manor governed by trust lords elected by the freeholders.

MUKER (YNR), the former lead-mining capital of upper Swaledale, is a village of entrancing irregularity with a primitive-looking church, and sturdy and perhaps rather dour cottages of the dark grey Pennine gritstone. It stands in a very beautiful part of the dale, clustered above the north bank of the river, and like many other villages of the dales, it has a background of the green valley side, seamed by becks and stone walls.

RIPLEY (YWR), though not in the Pennines proper, lies on the lower slopes west of the Vale of York on the Ripon–Harrogate road before this crosses the Nidd, and is a planned village of distinction. A street of houses built between about 1780 and 1860, in styles varying from Gothic to Tudor, leads to the little square, in the centre of which is a partly-medieval cross. On the west are the fourteenth- to sixteenth-century church and the fifteenth-century gatehouse giving access to the spacious courtyard of Ripley Castle, which has a sixteenth-century tower but is otherwise of about 1780.

WEST TANFIELD (YNR) is a most attractive village on the north bank of the Ure at the point where it is bridged by the road from Ripon to Wensleydale and where the river finally emerges from the hills. The fifteenth-century gatehouse, all that survives, of a castle of the Marmions, with its picturesque oriel window, and the restored

fifteenth-century church, which contains their alabaster effigies
and good woodwork by Robert Thompson of Kilburn, form a
delightful group on the river bank.

12 East of the Pennines

Most writers who attempt to describe some aspect of the English
scene are Southcountrymen who are not at ease in the six northern
counties. Their writing shows that they are happy in Cornwall or the
Cotswolds, on the Downs or in East Anglia, but when they cross
the Humber or the Mersey, it is all too evident that they have
entered unknown country. The natives, speaking a strange brogue,
seem unfriendly, if not actually hostile; and the landscape is for-
bidding if not repellent: they take a quick, superficial look and hurry
back to scenes more familiar and more intimate, away from the
'hard, industrial North'. They think it all as hard and uncompromising
as the Pennine gritstone, and all busy with steaming, sweating industry.
The villages here, they will tell you, are all the same—all 'hard, grey
and cold'.

If you don't believe me, hear what one of them has to say about it:
'. . . the villages of the North proclaim that here we have to do with a
different people and with a country which is far more a land apart than
any of the other regions of England . . . . Here men's greatest efforts
have been expended in a struggle with the elements, with the winds,
the cold, and the rugged soil. In making a covering for themselves
their only attempt has been to build firmly, and it has been hard to
build at all. Over nearly all these northern villages there is the same
impress of monotony.'

Well, I lived in the north for a good many years, and during not
very propitious times, either, but I never met a countryman who felt
that his greatest efforts were being expended in a struggle with the
elements. As for the villages all having the same impress of monotony,
I wonder what the villagers of Bishop Burton and Burnsall, Downham
and Harewood, Hawkshead and Troutbeck, Blanchland and Bamburgh
think of this.

As I mentioned earlier, the chalk and the limestone which form
those great stone belts sweeping across England come up to the surface
again in Yorkshire. But the idea that the villages of the East and North

Ridings are merely the poor relations of those built on the similar formations farther south (I stress this point again) is superficial in the extreme. As the chalk is geologically a continuation of the long belt breached by the Humber, the villages in this locality might be expected to have the same characteristics as those around the Wolds of Lincolnshire. But in fact the Yorkshire Wolds differ strikingly in character from those south of the Humber; they are bolder and better wooded and more intensively cultivated. The chalk itself is harder and more compact than the variety found farther south, say on the Chilterns or the South Downs; it has indeed more the consistency of limestone.

The Wolds are most prominent and best known where they fall to the sea at Flamborough Head and the fine sheer cliffs to the west towards Filey. The heights southward from here once enclosed a wide bay stretching round to reach the Humber upstream from Hull, but they now look out over the vast Plain of Holderness, which is not flat but rather irregular in surface. This was new land formed from the boulder clay deposited by the retreating glaciers at the end of the Ice Age, and as in Lincolnshire, there are many tracts of marshland and mere. The villages are mostly built of brick and often pleasantly whitewashed.

A brick-making industry, the earliest in England, had been established around Hull and Beverley since the early fourteenth century, no doubt stimulated by the trading connections of Hull with the Netherlands and the Baltic ports, among the most thriving regions of brick building. Brick was employed extensively in Beverley Minster and the large parish church of Holy Trinity at Hull, and it was used also to build a new clerestory for the village church of Roos, near Withernsea, but only gradually did it find its way into more humble buildings. These were often constructed of cobbles collected from the boulder clay and known locally as 'boulder stones'. The roofs in the villages today are frequently of pantiles, though occasionally of thatch.

The sea is kept out of the Plain of Holderness by a line of low soft cliffs of a reddish boulder clay. These are under constant attack by the waves, which have eaten away two miles or more during historic times, resulting in a loss not only of much good cultivable land but also of many villages. As if in compensation, new deposits are being laid down round the estuary of the Humber; the long bank of shingle which ends in Spurn Head is being pushed ever farther out and the Humber is slowly being filled up. The ancient village of Hedon, in this district, was once more important as a port than Hull, and its old docks can still be traced, but its magnificent church, the 'king of Holderness', now gazes out over flat fields to the Humber, which has retreated more than two miles.

On the Wolds there are no flint buildings such as those seen in East Anglia or on the Downs, but the chalk itself was once popular as a building material; quarries in the southern part flourished in the Middle Ages, and the one at North Newbald supplied stone for Beverley Minster in the thirteenth century. The chalk, which was comparatively easy to quarry, was normally shaped into large blocks and left for several years to dry out. But here again the demand for chalk declined with the growth in popularity of brick.

Between the chalk and the limestone farther north, there is a tract of really level land, the Vale of Pickering. This remarkable piece of landscape, extending over 30 miles from Helmsley, on the edge of the moors, to the sea at Filey, and about four to eight miles across, was originally a great lake, created by the glacial clay holding up the eastward-flowing rivers. The floor of this vanished lake is covered by layers of clay and silt, a marshy region which has been drained only in recent years and is now given over to cattle pasturage. The low islands in the former marshland support several villages, but more of these, and they include some of the pleasantest villages in Yorkshire, are to be found along the margin, which is higher and drier land, especially where the rivers descending from the moorland dales have formed small deltas.

As the Yorkshire Wolds differ from the chalklands farther south, so the limestones of the North Yorkshire Moors differ markedly from those of the great oolitic belt. In fact, most people wouldn't recognise them as limestones at all. Unlike the Cotswolds, whose surface is of sweet green grass, or the pastures of the Northamptonshire uplands, the limestone country of North Yorkshire is a huge tract of uncultivated heather-covered moorland. Bearing indeed a greater resemblance to the Pennines, it reaches well over 1,000 feet in many places and is dissected by numerous deep and narrow dales.

The beds of rocks are thinner in this hilly region than in the Cotswolds or even in Lincolnshire; they consist of an intermixture of liassic stones (ironstones and limestones) with gritstones and shales.

In consequence, there is a greater diversity in the strata, resulting in a richer variety in the landscape. Apart from the Esk, which descends eastward to Whitby, practically all the longer dales, secluded and beautifully wooded, run down to the Vale of Pickering. Elsewhere, the moorlands break away sharply in steep escarpments where the harder rocks appear; on the northern side in the Cleveland Hills, on the west in the Hambleton Hills, facing out over the fertile Vale of York. On the moors themselves, as in the Pennines, there are practically no settlements, but many delightful villages can be found in the dales. The native limestone, which varies from light grey to light brown in colour, is used very effectively in building here (and also finds its way out into the Vale of York) and red tiles everywhere add colour to the scene.

On their seaward side the Yorkshire Moors end in great upstanding cliffs, the highest in England. Here the layers of grey shales, brown gritstones and variegated limestones can be well seen. The clays have worn down more rapidly and more consistently than the harder rocks, causing a wide diversity in the shapes and colours of the cliff formations. These fascinating irregularities have lent charm to the entrancingly-situated fishing villages, with roofs of warm red tiles, to be seen perched on ledges or set in deep ravines along the coast. Some of these villages are first heard of only in late medieval times. Staithes, for example, is first mentioned in 1415; its name means nothing more than 'landing place' and it originated as a harbour for the older villages of Seaton and Hinderwell inland. None of these fishing villages was of any significance until the curious and sudden expansion of the industry in the fifteenth century.

From the southern end of the Hambleton Hills, the limestone pushes out a long extension (the Howardian Hills) that effectively shut in the primeval lake in the Vale of Pickering. This long tongue of land is separated from the Wolds only by the narrow passage which the Derwent decided to make (to the Vale of York) when the river discovered it couldn't find a way out through the glacial barrier to the sea. The Vale of York (or Mowbray, as it used to be called) is a wide undulating tract of alluvial clays, not remarkable for its villages, enclosed on the east by a thin strip of New Red Sandstone. The position of York itself, in the centre of the vale, is marked by an outcrop of this sandstone. The west of the vale is fringed by a long band of

Magnesian Limestone, of great value as a building stone (quarries at Tadcaster, for instance, supplied the stone for York Minster). The band actually stretches north from Nottingham right across Yorkshire to the coast of Durham and we shall find that it is of greater significance in the next section.

Villages East of the Pennines

BISHOP BURTON (YER), where the road from Beverley to Market Weighton and York reaches the Wolds, is the most charming village in east Yorkshire. The road drops into a secluded hollow and curves round a large crescent-shaped pond, backed by trees, beyond which, on a hillock, rises the squat thirteenth-century tower of the picturesque church. On the other side of the road is the village green, planted with fine chestnut trees, with characteristic white cottages grouped around it.

BISHOP WILTON (YER) is a delightful village at the foot of the steep western escarpment of the Wolds, south of the road from York to Driffield. Its houses, of brick, many of them colour-washed and with pantiled roofs, line two roads on either side of a wide green down the centre of which bubbles and gurgles a beck. A little to the north rises the tall fourteenth-century spire of the church, and beyond is a green background of the wolds, clad here and there with woods.

COXWOLD (YNR), on a ridge facing the gap between the Hambleton Hills and the Howardians, is a very attractive village, mostly of one broad street. Its stone houses, bordering long strips of grass, run up to the fifteenth-century church, which has a remarkable tower, octagonal from the ground. Laurence Sterne was perpetual curate here in 1760-8 and wrote part of *Tristram Shandy* and *A Sentimental Journey* in the seventeenth-century house now called Shandy Hall, at the west end of the village.

CRAYKE (YNR) is a fascinating brick-built village in a commanding situation on the slope and summit of a hill, an outlying spur of the Howardians, east of the York to Thirsk road at Easingwold. Two roads ascend from the plain to meet at a junction from which a third, wide street, with margins of green, ascends the backbone of the spur to the fifteenth-century church and fourteenth- to fifteenth-century castle ruins at the top. From this point there is a

38 *Dufton, Westmorland*
39 *Langtoft, Yorkshire East Riding*

wonderful view over the Vale of York, with the towers of the Minster in the distance.

GANTON (YER) is one of a line of attractive villages at the foot of the Wolds between Malton and Filey, facing northward over the Vale of Pickering to the North Yorkshire Moors. The main street, which has a clear chalk beck running down the side, is made pleasant by cottages of whitewashed stone, roofed with red pantiles and backed by trees. Above these rises the tower and tall octagonal spire of the church, which is chiefly of the fifteenth century.

GOATHLAND (YNR) is a singularly delightful moorland village west of the road from Whitby to Pickering and on a plateau between two becks that join a little below it to form a tributary of the Esk. The village farmsteads, with their weathered pantile roofs, are scattered about a large open common, with the fine church of 1896 at the south end. Goathland, which has long been visited for its waterfalls (the nearest is Mallyan Spout, just below the village on the west), has grown into quite a holiday place (of the better kind) in recent years.

KILBURN (YNR), in a valley below Roulston Scar, at the southern end of the Hambleton Hills, and south of the Helmsley–Thirsk road, is a very pleasant village which has a church remarkable for its Norman work and a long street of stone cottages (one has a timber-framed upper storey) with flower-filled gardens, separated from the road on one side by a stream. Robert Thompson, whose very fine wood-carving (his 'signature' was a mouse) enriches many Yorkshire churches, had his village workshop here.

LANGTON (YER), to the south of Malton, is well known for its race-horses, which are trained on Langton Wold, a long plateau of the chalk extending from the Wolds and enclosing the village on the north. The cottages, which have an air of refinement about them, are nearly all of grey stone, with roofs of pantiles or slate. The central part of the village faces south over a wide trim green, with a lovely view of the curving wood-fringed Wolds beyond.

LASTINGHAM (YNR) is on the southern slopes of the North Yorkshire Moors, between the beautiful glens of Farndale and Rosedale and some distance from the road between Kirkby Moorside and Pickering. It is a delightful village with an exceptionally interesting

40 *Blanchland, Northumberland*

church, on what has been called one of the most sacred sites in ancient Northumbria. Below the late-twelfth-century nave is an aisled Norman crypt of about 1080 which is almost a lower church. From the moors above the head of the village there is a splendid view over the Vale of Pickering to the Wolds.

NORTH NEWBALD (YER), lying just east of the road from Hull to Market Weighton which runs below the escarpment of the Wolds, has another most interesting Norman church. This is at the south end of the village, whose main street, lined by houses with fronts of stone, brick and colour-wash, and pantiled roofs, follows the course of a little beck up to a green, then climbs the scarp slope to a larger green, sheltered by tall trees.

PATRINGTON (YER), where the road from Hull to Withernsea turns away from that going on towards Spurn Head, had a harbour in Leland's time, but now stands in flat fields north of the Humber. This large village is famous for its beautiful cruciform church, the 'queen of Holderness', an exquisite example of the fourteenth-century or Decorated style, and one of the most perfect parish churches in England. The noble central tower and spire, over 180 feet high, can be seen for many miles across the plain.

ROBIN HOOD'S BAY (YNR), near the northern end of the large and beautiful bay between Whitby and Scarborough from which it takes its present name (it was formerly called Bay Town), is a picturesque village perched irregularly on a steep slope descending towards the sea, in an amphitheatre of hills that sweep down from the North Yorkshire Moors. The red-tiled roofs of its houses contrast effectively with the grey stone walls, the deep brown of the cliffs and the blue-green of the sea. Long engaged in the coastal shipping trade, the village is now dependent principally on its holiday visitors.

STAITHES (YNR), another picturesque coastal village, once an important centre of herring fishing, is between Whitby and Saltburn. It lies at the foot of a deep ravine, along either side of a beck which reaches the sea through a narrow break in the cliffs, and is approached by a precipitous descent. Staithes is completely hidden from the plateau of the surrounding country and even from the tops of the neighbouring cliffs, of which that to the west, Boulby Cliff, is the highest in England.

WELTON (YER) is just north of the road from Hull to Selby and Market Weighton, on the southern slopes of the Wolds and facing out across the broad Humber to the flat landscape of Lincolnshire. Its pleasant houses are mostly built round an attractive green, with a willow-fringed pool banked up below the churchyard wall. Behind the church, which is partly of the late fifteenth century, though much restored, is a glimpse of the charmingly wooded scarp face of the wolds.

13 North-East England

The villages of the two north-eastern counties, taken as a whole, show very considerable divergences from those of the region on their southern boundary, though this is not evident immediately you cross the Tees. The villages of South Durham, indeed, look very much like those of North Yorkshire, and this is not surprising, for the country on either side of the river is very similar. The Tees forms a natural geographical boundary, but there is no geological distinction here. A belt of the reddish-brown Keuper Sandstones that comes to light in the neighbourhood of Boroughbridge and extends over the northern part of the Vale of York, sweeps round the foot of the Cleveland Hills to the estuary of the Tees. In this sandstone region, on both sides of the river, are some excellent little villages; the houses are plain and eminently practical, it is true, but they are mostly enlivened by white-wash and red tiles, and nearly all stand at the fringes of generous greens. Like all the best villages, these seem to fit naturally into the landscape.

To the west of the sandstone stretches the long and at first comparatively narrow belt of Magnesian Limestone I mentioned in the last section. Crossed by the Tees upstream from Darlington, it spreads out over County Durham to end in the steep yellowish-brown cliffs that form almost all the coast between Hartlepool and South Shields. The cliffs are broken up by attractive little 'denes' through which the streams escape to the sea, and some of the old villages stand at the sides of these. Inland, the Magnesian Limestone forms the line of hills that has forced the river Wear to take a northward course, involving it in intricate folds round the great cathedral and castle of Durham.

The limestone is in reality a thick bed of dolomite, with a considerable proportion of magnesium carbonate in its make up. As I said earlier, it is of great value for building, and the best stone (mostly from quarries in Yorkshire) was employed in many of the great churches and abbeys of the north-east. The crystalline texture of the limestone gives it a lively brightness when it is newly quarried; unfortunately, it not only hardens, but it darkens and tends to crumble on exposure to the weather, and in the atmosphere of the industrial districts of County Durham it has not stood up well to the elements (though these are by no means as smoky or chemical-laden as formerly) and the villages here tend to look drab and poor, quite apart from the unhappy intrusion of Victorian brick.

Around the lower courses of the Wear and the Tyne we have a resurgence of the Coal Measures, forming the Northumberland and Durham coalfield (though they take up a very small part of Northumberland). The idea that coal workings must necessarily turn the landscape into a depressingly dull grey-black smudge is of course nonsense. There is a considerable diversity of rocks in the coalfield, lending variety to the villages; among the shales and softer deposits occur thick layers of sandstone, and this has been used a great deal in the older buildings (Washington Hall and George Stephenson's cottage at Wylam are typical examples).

The Coal Measures are bounded on the west by a strip of Millstone Grit, the tough, durable buff-tinted stone from which, though difficult to work, has also been used to some extent. But the most important outcrop east of the Pennines in this region is that of the Fell Sandstone, a sedimentary rock of the Carboniferous group. It begins on the north in the Kyloe Hills, inland from Holy Island, runs south towards the Aln (one of the only two rivers to cut through it), and then sweeps away south-west towards the North Tyne in a great range of heather-covered moorland, reaching nearly 1,500 feet in the Simonside Hills. The Coquet, the other river penetrating the sandstone, winds through a valley of incomparable beauty, with many delectable small villages in charming settings.

The Fell Sandstone, too, has given up its rock for village building—in fact, Northumberland is pre-eminently a region of sandstone building. I mentioned in the section on the Pennines that the Carboniferous or Mountain Limestone extended across the Tyne Gap to the Cheviots, but that its quality changed. Here the strata are thinly bedded and the rock is more in the nature of sandstone than limestone, owing to the preponderance of grains of silica in its structure. This stone is extremely strong and durable; it does not lend itself much to architectural ornament, though it can show some surprisingly delicate colours in its shades of grey, buff and light brown. Wallington Hall, the home of the Trevelyans, is a very good example of what can be done with this sandstone, but it is the common building material of numerous quiet and unspoilt villages over a wide area of Northumberland.

North of the Tyne Gap, the Mountain Limestone forms a broad moorland range covered with heather and coarse grass, and the villages, mostly small and far apart (though none the less attractive for that) are confined to the long, enticing valleys, especially those of the North and South Tynes. The range increases in height until it reaches the great domed moorlands, mostly over 2,000 feet high, of the Cheviot Hills, crossed by the Scottish Border. Here the rocks are forced apart by several kinds of granitic intrusion, one of which, the hard red porphyry, has been much used for road surfacing.

Across the moorlands just north of the Tyne Gap stretches the long line of crags that carries the great Wall of Hadrian. It shows a bold scarp face to the north and from its crest the rolling grasslands are seen reaching away endlessly to the Border. Dark blue-grey or even black when weathered, this outcrop, known as the Great Whin Sill, is in fact formed by the intrusion of an igneous rock, a basalt composed by being injected in a molten state into faults in the existing rock structure and then crystallised. The great dark crags are a measure of its resistance to erosion.

The earliest builders in this wild country—the Roman legionaries—knew the value of the natural rampart created by this wall of rock. They also appreciated the value of the local grey-brown sandstones from the Mountain Limestone formations, using them everywhere for facing their great defence work. The medieval builders followed their example and 'borrowed' stones from the Wall and other Roman works for their churches, villages, farms and pele-towers. Inscribed stones from *Corstopitum*, for instance, can be seen in the houses of the near-by village, Corbridge. The pele-tower, a fortified dwelling built as a defence against the pillaging Scots,* was

* See my *Scottish Border Country*, p. 26.

a necessity for almost every village within striking distance of the Border before the Union of 1603. The Great Whin Sill also juts up in other places: it forms the headland on which Dunstanburgh Castle is built and the huge upstanding crag which supports the massive Bamburgh Castle and protects the village of Bamburgh from the sea. This exceptionally hard rock was too difficult to quarry for building stone, and the castle keep at Bamburgh is actually built of sandstone brought here by sea.

The Pennine moorlands south of the Tyne Gap form the link between the Northumbrian moors and the Yorkshire Pennines, the northern reaches of which they resemble to some extent. The higher part consists of desolate and lonely heathlands with occasional rough pastures. Along their western edge, where they attain a height of over 2,000 feet, the moorlands end in a long unbroken escarpment facing over the Eden valley, but eastward they descend easily to the finely-wooded country, split up by many intricate valleys, on the frontiers of the Durham coalfield.

The moorlands are trenched by long, deep valleys, like those of the upper Wear and of the Derwent which forms the boundary with Northumberland for some distance. Along these the margins of cultivation and consequently the lines of villages run well up into the barren land. The fields are divided by grey-brown sandstone walls, and here and there are the grey-brown buildings of the farms and small villages. Sandstone is also the natural roofing material throughout the moorland districts of the north-east; the huge roofing slabs are often more than an inch thick, imposing a weight on the structure which sometimes the supporting timbers can hardly stand. During the past century, however, stone roofs here, as elsewhere, have mostly been superseded by slates imported from Wales or the Lake District, with a consequent loss in that harmony with the landscape which the indigenous building materials achieve.

Villages of North-East England

BAMBURGH (Nb), the Saxon capital of Northumbria from the sixth to the mid-eighth century, is now a secluded and colourful village of grey stone cottages, mostly of the eighteenth and early nineteenth centuries and gathered round a wooded green. It is dominated by the magnificent castle, which with its huge Norman keep crowns the top of the immense basaltic crag rising directly from the foot of the village and sheltering it from the sea. At the upper end of the village is the church, mainly of the twelfth and thirteenth centuries and one of the finest in the Border Country.

BLANCHLAND (Nb) is an enchanting village in the sequestered and richly wooded valley of the upper Derwent. Remains of the Premonstratensian abbey founded here in 1165 survive in the tower and chancel of the parish church and are built into the planned village which is romantically entered either by a bridge across the river from County Durham or through the original abbey gateway of about 1500. The charming houses of grey-brown stone, with stone-slab roofs, were built after 1752 round the L-shaped square, with the Lord Crewe Arms (formed out of thirteenth-century ruins) on the west.

CORBRIDGE (Nb), on the north bank of the stony Tyne, downstream from Hexham, succeeded Bamburgh as the capital of Northumbria. The church, though mostly of the thirteenth century (when Corbridge was a flourishing town), has an unusual Saxon porch-tower with an arch, brought in its entirety, probably in the eighth century, from the Roman town of *Corstopitum* near by. At the edge of the churchyard is a fourteenth-century pele-tower also built with Roman stones and intended as a refuge for the priest. The Angel Inn is of the seventeenth century (with later additions) and there are other charming houses of the same period in the village.

EGGLESCLIFFE (Du) is delightfully situated on the high north bank of the Tees, overlooking the little town of Yarm, on the Yorkshire side. Round the tree-shaded green and the fifteenth-century church, east of the road from Stockton, are grouped the picturesque houses, some of the eighteenth century and mostly of a reddish-brown brick. Lower down, the main road crosses the river by a bridge of about 1400, and farther west is a lofty railway viaduct of 43 brick arches, built in 1849.

ELSDON (Nb), to the north of the road from Newcastle to Edinburgh by way of Jedburgh, has a variety of eighteenth-century and other houses, built round a large green on the edge of the rolling moors that stretch without interruption to the Scottish Border. On the green is the fourteenth-century church, and above stands the

embattled rectory, built about 1400 and the most outstanding
example of this kind of fortification in the Border. The curious
twin motte-hills near the Rothbury road probably once supported
a Norman castle.

ETAL (Nb), on the road from Wooler to Berwick, is an unusually
pretty village consisting of a single street of whitewashed cottages,
mostly of one storey, some with thatched roofs (uncommon in the
Border) and some having roofs of large, grey slabs—the whole
surrounded by trees in the most delightful manner. The street
leads in one direction to the fourteenth-century ruins of the
castle, and on the other side of the main road to the eighteenth-
century manor house.

GAINFORD (Du), which lies mostly between the Darlington to Barnard
Castle road and the Tees, is an engaging village, the stone cottages
of the older part set round an irregularly-shaped green attractively
planted with trees. At the south-west angle of the green is the
excellent early-thirteenth-century church, of mellow grey stone,
charmingly positioned close to the river bank, and farther west is
the Hall, a well-restored stone house dating from about 1600.
Near this is a large circular dovecot, also of stone.

HOLY ISLAND (Nb), the birthplace of English Christianity, where St
Aidan established a bishopric in 635, is reached from the mainland
by a causeway across the sands, which are dry only at low tide. It
is chiefly visited on account of the beautiful warm red sandstone
ruins of the Benedictine priory of Lindisfarne, founded in early
Norman times; but the grey, windswept fishing village is also of
interest and has a church of the late twelfth and thirteenth centuries. To the west, on a steep basaltic outcrop, rises the romantic
Lindisfarne Castle, built about 1500 to protect the harbour and
converted into a private residence by Sir Edwin Lutyens.

HURWORTH-ON-TEES (Du) is a handsome village with a green ½-mile
long and houses occupied in the eighteenth century by the merchants of Darlington. It stands on a high bank above a pleasant reach
of the Tees and its gardens slope down to the river, from which the
red roofs of the houses and the much-restored church, with its
fifteenth-century tower, show to picturesque effect. Hurworth is
extended on the east by NEASHAM, another notable village likewise
overlooking a fine reach of the Tees.

MITFORD (Nb), which lies upstream from Morpeth and is approached through a verdant glen, is a small but charming village delightfully situated near the confluence of the Font with the Wansbeck, their clear waters mingling over sandstone beds beneath steep, wooded banks. Farther on, over the hill, in a sequestered position surrounded by woodlands, are the church, with a thirteenth-century chancel and a distinctive spire of 1875, and the ruins of the twelfth-century castle, on a mound above the Wansbeck.

NORHAM (Nb) is in a lovely position on the south side of the Tweed, facing across the broad river into Scotland. It has a long, irregular street of grey stone cottages lining each side of a spacious green on which stands the village cross, partly medieval. To the north is the church, with splendid Norman work in the chancel and south arcade, and at the east end of the village rise the beautiful pink sandstone ruins of the castle, the imposing Border stronghold of the prince-bishops of Durham, built round a massive keep of the twelfth century.

NORTON (Du), though to all outward appearances a suburb of Stockton, is in fact the remarkably complete and unspoilt survival of an eighteenth-century residential village. It consists wholly of one long street with a welcome avenue of trees and many notable houses, leading north from the Billingham road to the green, adjacent to which are the fine eighteenth-century vicarage and the church, one of the most interesting in the county. This has a Saxon crossing tower and excellent work of the twelfth to fifteenth centuries.

PIERCEBRIDGE (Du), on the south side of the road from Darlington to Barnard Castle, is very unusual in being built on a Roman site. It stands within the ramparts (partly revealed) of a third-century fort placed to guard the point where the road from York to *Corstopitum* crossed the Tees. The present stately bridge, a little to the east, dates from 1789. The village of low whitewashed and red-tiled cottages is mostly arranged round a spacious green planted with trees.

WARKWORTH (Nb), one of the most enchantingly situated villages in England, stands on a narrow peninsula almost encircled by the Coquet, which runs below sandstone cliffs in a deep-set glen. The village is best approached on the north across the fortified fourteenth-century bridge. Near the river is the church, a remarkably complete Norman structure, and from the market place the main street, with eighteenth-century terraces, rises steeply to the neck of the peninsula, which is defended by the splendid ruins of the great castle of the Percys, chiefly of the thirteenth century, but with an unusual fifteenth-century keep.

WHALTON (Nb), which lies some distance north of Belsay on the Newcastle–Jedburgh road, in quiet pastoral country, is a very pleasing well-built village with a church of the twelfth and thirteenth centuries and a broad street of brown stone cottages standing behind flowery gardens on either side of a green. The manor house, at the east end, was converted in 1909 by Sir Edwin Lutyens, who linked up four of the village houses. On 4th July (old Midsummer's Eve) the villagers still kindle a bonfire and dance round it—perhaps a relic of pagan worship!

14 North-West England

When one speaks of the north-west of England—the last section of our all-too-rapid regional survey—most people probably think only of the Lake District, that incomparable cartwheel of mountains, dales and lakes reaching from Windermere to Skiddaw and from Ullswater to Eskdale. The scenery of the Lake District is so well known and has been so often and so eloquently described in poetry and prose that there is no need for me to dwell on it here, much as I would like to. Our business is with villages, and this relatively small and extremely compact region is not only of interest for its scenery, which attracts everyone, it has a history and a way of life that mark it off from other regions.

But the Lake District, though it may be the hub of the north-west, is not all of it. We have already looked across to this country from the edge of the Pennine moorlands and may have been impressed by the variety of the scenery spread out before us. What we may not have realised is that the basic cause of that variety, and the variety we find in the villages, is the great diversity in the rock structure. Only as we move about the region do we appreciate the strong contrasts between the grey Pennine limestone, the red sandstones of the Vale of Eden and the Cumberland coast, the dark volcanic rocks of the central Lakeland massif, the white mountain limestone of the southern fringe round that fascinating area, and the grey-brown millstone grit of much of north Lancashire.

It is not generally appreciated either that nearly all these outcrops provide building stones of various qualities and uses. If the Lake District, for instance, is thought of at all as a region of building materials, it is as a provider of slates for roofs and to a more limited extent for the walls of the local buildings. But I will come back to this, after dealing with the other parts of the north-west.

From the unbroken escarpment of their western edge, the Pennine moors fall away steeply to the long, deep trough of the Vale of Eden, a lovely pastoral glen cut through an outcrop of the New Red Sandstone which runs down past Carlisle towards the Solway Firth and the flat north coast of Cumberland. All along the vale and over north Cumberland are pleasant villages in which the sandstone has been used to good effect. The New Red Sandstone spreads across the lower valley of the Irthing and round the mountain limestone of the Border hills; it is a noticeable feature, for example, not only in the beautiful priory ruins of Lanercost but also in the charming little village, for which some of the stones were taken from the Roman Wall close by.

The red sandstone also extends up the coast of Lancashire across the level plain of The Fylde (a rich agricultural area this, with some pleasant, quiet villages) and reappears in the peninsula of Furness on the north side of Morecambe Bay, from which it goes on up the coast of Cumberland. The sandstone from St Bees Head and other outcrops in this neighbourhood is of particular importance for building; it is consistently strong and durable, and it shows a considerable variety of colour, ranging from a deep salmon-red to an equally deep peach-yellow. It is well seen in the ruins of Furness Abbey, near Barrow, but it also found its way into many village buildings, into their churches in particular. This sandstone is separated from that of north Cumberland by a small tract of the Coal Measures, around White-haven, which has made as much mess of the older villages as the much larger areas in Lancashire and Yorkshire.

Round the head of Morecambe Bay and along the southern outskirts of Lakeland are numerous outcrops of the Mountain Limestone, familiar to all who have approached the inner sanctum from the south. They show themselves as long, precipitous scars of an amazing whiteness and contribute to the delightful scenery round the estuaries of the Kent and

Leven, as well as to the village building. This was a flourishing sheep-rearing district in the Middle Ages; a clothmaking industry believed to have been started in the fourteenth century by the Flemings (a name still found hereabouts) was centred in Kendal, and the serge known as 'Kendal green' became famous. Another strip of the Mountain Limestone, running out from the Pennines south of Kirkby Stephen, extends by way of the Shap Fells and round 'the back o' Skidda' towards Cockermouth. Here the tones of the building stones are warmer, varying from white to a soft grey and even a light brown which makes itself felt in the villages of this locality. It is difficult to realise that aeons ago in geological time, the Mountain Limestone completely covered the rocks of Lakeland, but after the great eruptions in the centre it was worn away and now forms only a broken ring round the outside.

This brings us back to the Lake District proper, which is unique in the English scene and also has a pattern of settlement different from that of any other region. In the tenth century, mainly, Norwegian invaders sailed up the Solway and the estuaries of Furness and established themselves in the dales. Before their coming, the dale bottoms had been marshy and difficult to cultivate; the Celtic inhabitants lived on the fell sides or on level places on the moorlands (where traces of their settlements can still be seen). But the Norsemen, with the better implements they had at their command, cleared and drained the dales, began their cultivation and founded their farmsteads and small villages. Evidence of this settlement still survives in the village names—Rydal, Grasmere, Hawkshead, Coniston, Seathwaite, Wasdale, Buttermere, Rosthwaite, Threlkeld and Patterdale—all these contain Old Norse elements.

Characteristic of the settlements that have never expanded is Wasdale Head, beyond the upper end of Wastwater on the west side of the Lake District. The little village, if it can be called that, is enclosed by small walled fields which make a bright patch of green on the dale floor, in striking contrast with the dark, craggy fells of Yewbarrow, Kirk Fell, Great Gable and Lingmell that crowd it in on almost every side. Isolated hamlets and tiny villages, invariably built of the local stone, are hidden away in many lonely recesses of the dales. Within the mountain area, the villages have nearly all remained small, even where they have developed into tourist centres. The dales themselves are cultivated only to a limited extent, but where they open out at the margins of Lakeland there is wider scope for agriculture and here we find the old market towns and larger villages, which show their greater affluence in their style of building.

Village building in and around the Lake District displays the characteristic features of the mountain districts of the north. The houses are built low and without ornament, but are frequently whitewashed; the roofs are of shallow pitch, no doubt better to withstand the elements, the roof ridges are unbroken from end to end, and the deep eaves characteristic of the south are rarely to be seen. A peculiarity of the Lake District are the massive round tapered chimneys, particularly to be noticed on the farmhouses. The church architecture is mostly straightforward and sparing of adornment; churches were 'for duration built, not raised in nice proportion', as Wordsworth said of Grasmere. The towers are frequently low and sturdy as though intended for defence, as indeed many of them were. From the fourteenth century until the Union with Scotland many pele-towers were built in the north-west, especially as the Eden and Kent valleys became cultivated, and they are still a feature of some villages.

All this may seem to paint a grim picture, but the rebuilding which affected all the northern counties from about 1690 onwards (about a century later, in fact, than the midlands and the south) showed itself also around the Lake District, and many villages and farmhouses were rebuilt from about this time. The reason perhaps was that these villages had been able to settle down at last after the cessation of the turmoil caused by the Border forays, and the improvements introduced into agriculture were now resulting in a higher standard of living. In their settings, too, the villages of the Lake counties were improved by the hand of man; they are frequently sheltered by sycamore trees, which had been introduced into England late in the sixteenth century. In the qualities of grouping and setting, the villages in and around the Lake District yield nothing to those of any part of England.

I have not said anything so far about the geological structure of the Lake District which has had such an important influence on village building. It is extremely complex, but if I can reduce the geology to simple terms, as I have tried to do throughout this book, I may say that the pattern resolves itself into three groups or rather bands running east and west across the district. On the north are the Skiddaw

Slates, which are not very slatey but include various grits and sandstones; in the centre are the volcanic rocks known as the Borrowdale
series which account for Scafell Pike and many other craggy peaks; and
on the south are rocks belonging to the Silurian system which we met
in the Western Marches, comprising grits and limestones and to some
extent like the Skiddaw formations. After these strata had been laid
down, they were subjected to intense volcanic activity. Thick beds
of lava together with rocks formed from the volcanic ash were thrown
out and these now make up the Borrowdale series. The immense earth
pressures imposed on the strata twisted the formations into a complicated structure, at the same time squeezing some of the sedimentary
deposits into slates.

Some hard things have been said by lovers of buildings and landscape
about slate—but I must say the strictures are mainly aimed at the mass-
produced, thin, dull-grey Welsh slates. In their colouring and texture,
I insist, the roofing slates of the Lake District yield pride of place
to no others. The slate-producing region of Lakeland extends over
practically all the district, from Kirkby-in-Furness north to Keswick,
as the walker will have noticed from the numerous quarries and their
unfortunate debris. What he may not have noticed is the diversity in
the colouring of the slates. Those quarried in the southern part of
Furness are mainly of a rather sombre grey-blue, but as we move north
to the quarries around Coniston we find slates of a rich variety of
greens, from a very light tone to a deep olive. Farther north again, the
Langdale and Elterwater slates are mostly a light green. The quarries
around Buttermere and Borrowdale, of which those overlooking the
Honister Pass are the best known, provide slates which vary from a
rich olive to a dark green-grey; these are the slates seen in the villages
around Keswick. The Skiddaw slates, never much used in building,
are mostly a dark grey.

Local slate had been used for roofing in the Lake District from early
times. Like the Welsh slate, it splits easily into slabs, but the individual slates, though fine in grain, are seldom as smooth or thin as
their Welsh counterparts. A roof of Lakeland slates, though both
thinner and lighter than a comparative roof of sandstone or limestone,
to which in truth it bears a greater resemblance, is considerably
heavier than one of Welsh slates. Like the Cotswold stone slates, those
of the Lake District are usually graded in size from the ridge to the

eaves. Often they can be seen hung on the walls as well; the slate-hung fronts we found in the South-West (Section 8) are a feature also of the Lake District.

The slate-stone was once quarried very extensively for building and it can be seen in a great many villages in the Lake District. This stone, naturally thicker and heavier than the roofing slate, is rough, hard and durable, and its colour is mostly a very dark green or black. Hence, by itself, it tends to convey a rather drab impression. But it was frequently combined with chunks of hard volcanic ash which had been carried down from the mountains during the Ice Age and could be readily collected from the becks or even from the fields. This intractable material, known locally as 'cobble stone', was greatly favoured for the building of field-walls and barns and also of houses. It was often laid dry (that is, without mortar) and when so laid it presents a rugged, rough-hewn appearance that seems not out of keeping with the sturdy and independent character of the dalesman.

No buildings, indeed, seem to fit so well into their natural mountain environment. Because of this, the National Park Planning Board have adopted the practice in any new or reconstructed buildings of keeping the mortar back from the surface of the walls to give the impression of dry-stone walling. It is in such ways, I feel sure, that the more enlightened builders and planners are maintaining the true tradition of building in our English villages.

Villages of North-West England

ASKHAM (We), on the west side of the Lowther valley, is reached from the Kendal–Penrith road by a public road across Lowther Park, from which it is separated by the river. The white seventeenth-century cottages of the very charming village border two long greens sloping up from the direction of the bridge and shaded by huge trees. Near the foot is Askham Hall, incorporating a pele-tower of the fourteenth century but otherwise mostly rebuilt after 1574, and close to the Lowther is the dignified church, rebuilt in 1833.

CARTMEL (La), a characteristic old market centre in a peaceful valley among the uplands north-west of Grange-over-Sands, is chiefly visited on account of its splendid and interesting Priory Church. Founded in the twelfth century for Augustinian canons, this has fine woodwork and an unusual tower, the upper stage of which is curiously at an angle to the lower. In the little square are the Priory Gatehouse, of the fourteenth century, and the eighteenth-century market cross.

CONISTON (La), in a grand position between Coniston Water and the range of the Furness Fells which culminates in the Coniston Old Man, has been left practically unmolested by the tourist industry. It was in fact better known in the nineteenth century, probably because of its associations with John Ruskin, who lived at Brantwood, on the other side of the lake, and is buried in the churchyard. The Ruskin Museum, in the Ambleside road, contains also local material of interest. The fifteenth-century Coniston Hall, now a farmhouse, south of the village and near the lake, was formerly the principal house of the Fleming family.

GRANGE-IN-BORROWDALE (Cu) lies beyond the head of Derwentwater, at the entrance to the magnificent dale, the most beautiful in the Lake District, with richly-coloured fells rising on either hand. Here a deep pool of the Derwent is crossed by a much-photographed double bridge. The small but delightful village takes its name from a monastic farm of the Cistercians of Furness Abbey, who purchased land in the dale in the early thirteenth century.

GRASMERE (We), though inevitably affected in the summer season by the tourist trade, remains a genuine Lakeland village at heart, and its setting in the verdant vale of the Rothay could hardly be improved. Grasmere is of course most famous for its associations with William and Dorothy Wordsworth, who lived at Dove Cottage, a typical Lake country dwelling, near the charming mere, from 1799 to 1808; then moved to Allan Bank, a larger house above the village, and in 1811 to the Parsonage, opposite the rugged church, which dates partly from the thirteenth century. The Wordsworths are buried in the churchyard.

HAWKSHEAD (La), between Windermere and Coniston Water, is an exceptionally picturesque village, an intricate network of little squares and alleys connected by narrow passages and archways under the houses, some of which are slate-hung in the Lakeland fashion. Wordsworth, who attended the old Grammar School, founded in 1585, lodged at Ann Tyson's Cottage, a typical whitewashed dwelling in one of the alleys. The church, mainly of the sixteenth century (when Hawkshead was a busy clothmaking centre), is built of Silurian limestone and stands on a knoll above the village.

HORNBY (La) is beautifully situated on the Wenning, a tributary of the Lune, in the heart of the green Lonsdale, and is also on the road from Lancaster to Kirkby Lonsdale. The dignified village, built in the local red sandstone, is dominated by the noble keep of a castle (the rest of the building has been modernised). The keep, like the church with its unusual octagonal tower, was built by Sir Edward Stanley early in the sixteenth century. The church now has a nineteenth-century nave, but in the churchyard is an Anglian cross.

KENTMERE (We), in the secluded valley of the Kent which runs north from the Kendal–Windermere road, is built on a rib of rock above the site of the vanished mere. The pleasant village has seventeenth- and eighteenth-century houses gathered round the simple grey stone church (probably of the sixteenth century, but restored in 1866, when the tower was added). The picturesque Kentmere Hall, to the west, embowered in sycamores, was rebuilt in the late fifteenth century, except for the ruined fourteenth-century pele-tower attached to it.

MELMERBY (Cu), on the Penrith–Hexham road which climbs up from the Vale of Eden and over the Pennines, is a quiet village mostly scattered round a large green through which a beck flows, backed by the windswept moorland escarpment. It was a very remote place until the coach road was made early in the nineteenth century. The only outlet on the east before this was by a rough track which led over the moors of Hartside Fell to Alston.

RYDAL (We) is a charming village, scarcely more than a hamlet, on the road from Ambleside to Grasmere and near the foot of the delectable little Rydal Water, above which rises the precipitous crag of Nab Scar. Wordsworth lived from 1813 (when he left Grasmere) until his death, in 1850, at Rydal Mount, on the left of the steep, wooded lane above the church, and a field behind the church noted for its daffodils is named after his daughter, Dora. Rydal Hall, to the east of the village, was a seat of the Flemings rebuilt in the eighteenth century.

TEMPLE SOWERBY (We), one of the most delightful villages in the Vale of Eden, is on the road from Penrith to Appleby, below the dark western escarpment of the Pennines. It is chiefly grouped round two spacious greens, and its most interesting building is the red sandstone Manor House, which is partly of the sixteenth century, but mainly of the eighteenth. The village derives the first part of its name from the fact that the manor belonged to the Knights Templars in the thirteenth century.

TROUTBECK (We), above the Windermere–Patterdale road which climbs up to the Kirkstone Pass, is a particularly verdant village stretched along the steep side of Wansfell, with groups of characteristic cottages here and there, secluded among sycamores and apple trees. Townend, at the extreme southern end of the village, is a very charming early-seventeenth-century yeoman's house with a wealth of carved oak furniture of the same period.

WETHERAL (Cu), south of the Carlisle–Brampton road, is in a beautiful position on the west bank of the Eden, which is bordered here by lovely woods. On the large green is the old market cross, and facing across the river is a pele-like red sandstone gatehouse, all that remains of a Benedictine priory founded in 1106. A rowing-boat ferries across the river to Corby Castle, a seventeenth-century house built on to a thirteenth-century pele-tower. From the higher part of the river banks there are wide views across a level strath to Scotland—but that must be left for another day.

VILLAGES

in the Regional Survey arranged in order of Counties

(The numbers in brackets are those of the Sections
into which the Survey is divided)

BEDFORDSHIRE (Bd)
Elstow (6)
Old Warden (6)

BERKSHIRE (Bk)
Aldermaston (3)
Bray (3)
Buscot (6)
Coleshill (6)
East Hagbourne (2c)
East Hendred (2c)
Hurley (3)
Shrivenham (6)
Steventon (2c)
Sutton Courtenay (6)
Wargrave (3)

BUCKINGHAMSHIRE (Bu)
Bradenham (2c)
Brill (6)
Denham (3)
Fingest (2c)
Hambleden (2c)
Long Crendon (6)
Wendover (2c)
Weston Underwood (6)
West Wycombe (2c)

CAMBRIDGESHIRE (Ca)
Chippenham (5)
Fen Drayton (5)
Thorney (5)

CHESHIRE (Ch)
Prestbury (10b)
Styal (10b)

CORNWALL (Co)
Cadgwith (8b)
Mevagissey (8b)
Mousehole (8b)
Polperro (8b)
Port Isaac (8b)

St Breock (8b)
St Germans (8b)
Veryan (8b)

CUMBERLAND (Cu)
Grange-in-Borrowdale (14)
Melmerby (14)
Wetheral (14)

DERBYSHIRE (Db)
Castleton (11a)
Cromford (11a)
Eyam (11a)
Repton (10b)
Sudbury (10b)
Tideswell (11a)
Tissington (11a)
Winster (11a)

DEVONSHIRE (Dv)
Axmouth (8b)
Branscombe (8b)
Broadhembury (8b)
Clovelly (8a)
Cockington (8b)
Dittisham (8b)
Drewsteignton (8b)
Dunsford (8b)
Lynmouth (8a)
Manaton (8b)
Sampford Courtenay (8a)
Widecombe-in-the-Moor (8b)

DORSET (Dt)
Abbotsbury (7a)
Cerne Abbas (2b)
Corfe Castle (2b)
East Lulworth (2b)
Melbury Osmund (2b)
Milton Abbas (2b)

DURHAM (Du)
Egglescliffe (13)

Gainford (13)
Hurworth-on-Tees (13)
Neasham (*see* Hurworth)
Norton (13)
Piercebridge (13)

ESSEX (Ex)
Clavering (4)
Dedham (4)
Finchingfield (4)
Great Bardfield (4)
Hatfield Broad Oak (3)
Havering-atte-Bower (3)
Newport (4)
Terling (3)
Wivenhoe (3)

GLOUCESTERSHIRE (Gl)
Bibury (7b)
Bourton-on-the-Hill (7b)
Bourton-on-the-Water (7b)
Frampton-on-Severn (10a)
Lower Slaughter (7b)
Saintbury (7b)
Snowshill (7b)
Stanton (7b)
Stanway (7b)

HAMPSHIRE (Hp)
Beaulieu (2b)
Nether Wallop (2b)
Selborne (2b)
Southwick (2b)

HEREFORDSHIRE (He)
Bosbury (9)
Bredwardine (9)
Eardisland (9)
Eardisley (9)
Garway (9)
Pembridge (9)
Weobley (9)

HERTFORDSHIRE (Ht)
Aldbury (2c)
Ashwell (2c)
Much Hadham (3)
Westmill (3)

HUNTINGDONSHIRE (Hu)
Hemingford Grey (5)
Leighton Bromswold (5)

ISLE OF WIGHT (IW)
Godshill (2b)
Shorwell (2b)

KENT (Kt)
Aylesford (2a)
Biddenden (1)
Chiddingstone (1)
Chilham (2a)
Cobham (3)
Elham (2a)
Fordwich (3)
Goudhurst (1)
Groombridge (1)
Ightham (1)
Lamberhurst (1)
Lenham (2a)
Otham (1)
Penshurst (1)
Sutton Valence (1)

LANCASHIRE (La)
Cartmel (14)
Coniston (14)
Downham (11a)
Hawkshead (14)
Hornby (14)

LEICESTERSHIRE (Le)
Bottesford (10b)
Breedon-on-the-Hill (10b)
Hallaton (7c)

LINCOLNSHIRE (Li)
Bolingbroke (5)
Folkingham (5)
Fulbeck (5)
Greatford (5)
Somersby (5)

NORFOLK (Nf)
Castle Acre (4)
Castle Rising (4)
Horning (4)

NORTHAMPTONSHIRE (Np)
Ashby St Ledgers (7c)
Aynho (7c)
Barnwell (7c)
Colly Weston (7c)
Duddington (7c)
Geddington (7c)
Rockingham (7c)

NORTHUMBERLAND (Nb)
Bamburgh (13)
Blanchland (13)
Corbridge (13)
Elsdon (13)
Etal (13)
Holy Island (13)
Mitford (13)
Norham (13)
Warkworth (13)
Whalton (13)

NOTTINGHAMSHIRE (Nt)
Blyth (10b)
Linby (10b)

OXFORDSHIRE (Ox)
Adderbury (7c)
Bloxham (7c)
Burford (7b)
Cuxham (6)
Dorchester (6)
Ewelme (6)
Great Tew (7c)
Minster Lovell (7b)
Wroxton (7c)

RUTLAND (Rt)
Belton (7c)
Exton (7c)
Ketton (7c)
Lyddington (7c)

SHROPSHIRE (Sh)
Alveley (9)
Atcham (9)
Hodnet (10b)
Tong (10b)

SOMERSET (Sm)
Bossington (8a)
Croscombe (8a)
Dunster (8a)
East Coker (7a)
Hinton St George (7a)
Mells (7a)
Montacute (7a)
Muchelney (8a)
Nether Stowey (8a)
Norton St Philip (7a)
Porlock (8a)
Porlock Weir (see Porlock)
Queen Camel (7a)
Selworthy (8a)
Stogumber (8a)
Stoke-sub-Hamdon (7a)
Tintinhull (7a)

STAFFORDSHIRE (St)
Alton (11a)
Ilam (11a)

SUFFOLK (Sf)
Boxford (4)
Cavendish (4)
East Bergholt (4)
Hoxne (4)
Kersey (4)
Lavenham (4)
Long Melford (4)
Orford (4)
Stoke-by-Nayland (4)
Woolpit (4)

SURREY (Sy)
Betchworth (1)
Blechingley (1)
Chiddingfold (1)
Lingfield (1)
Shere (1)
Witley (1)

SUSSEX (Sx)
Alfriston (2a)
Amberley (2a)
Bosham (2b)

Bramber (2a)
Burwash (1)
Ditchling (1)
Lindfield (1)
Mayfield (1)
Northiam (1)
Sedlescombe (1)
South Harting (2a)
Steyning (2a)
Telscombe (2a)
West Dean (2a)
West Hoathly (1)

WARWICKSHIRE (Wa)
Bidford-on-Avon (10a)
Dunchurch (10a)
Ilmington (7b)
Meriden (10a)
Preston-on-Stour (10a)
Priors Marston (10a)
Stoneleigh (10a)
Tredington (10a)
Welford-on-Avon (10a)

WESTMORLAND (We)
Askham (14)
Grasmere (14)
Kentmere (14)
Rydal (14)
Temple Sowerby (14)
Troutbeck (14)

WILTSHIRE (Wt)
Aldbourne (2c)
Ashton Keynes (6)
Avebury (2c)
Biddestone (7b)
Castle Combe (7b)
Castle Eaton (6)
Chilmark (2b)
Lacock (7a)
Sherston Magna (7b)
Steeple Ashton (7a)
Stourton (7a)

WORCESTERSHIRE (Wo)
Bretforton (10a)

Broadway (7b)
Chaddesley Corbett (10a)
Cleeve Prior (10a)
Elmley Castle (10a)
Great Comberton (see Little Comberton)
Little Comberton (10a)
Norton (see Offenham)
Offenham (10a)

YORKSHIRE: EAST RIDING (YER)
Bishop Burton (12)
Bishop Welton (12)
Ganton (12)
Langton (12)
North Newbald (12)
Patrington (12)
Welton (12)

YORKSHIRE: NORTH RIDING (YNR)
Bainbridge (11b)
Castle Bolton (11b)
Coxwold (12)
Crayke (12)
Goathland (12)
Kilburn (12)
Lastingham (12)
Muker (11b)
Robin Hood's Bay (12)
Staithes (12)
West Tanfield (11b)

YORKSHIRE: WEST RIDING (YWR)
Bradfield (11a)
Burnsall (11b)
Delph (11a)
Dent (11b)
Dobcross (see Delph)
Giggleswick (11b)
Grassington (11b)
Harewood (11b)
Haworth (11a)
Heptonstall (11a)
Kettlewell (11b)
Ripley (11b)

NATIONAL TRUST

properties mentioned in the text (though not
necessarily referred to as such) :

Alfriston (2a): Clergy House
Atcham (9): Attingham Park
Avebury (2c): Avebury Circle
Bibury (7b): Arlington Row
Bosham (2b): Quay Meadow
Bossington (8a): village
Bradenham (2c): Manor House and village
Bramber (2a): Castle
Buscot (6): Buscot House and village
Cartmel (14): Priory Gatehouse
Cerne Abbas (2b): Cerne Giant
Chiddingstone (1): village
Cobham (3): Owletts
Coleshill (6): village
Dedham (4): *Shermans*
Goudhurst (1): *houses in village*
Grasmere (14): Allan Bank
Hawkshead (14): houses in village
Holy Island (13): Lindisfarne Castle
Ilam (11a): Ilam Hall and grounds
Lacock (7a): Lacock Abbey and village
Lavenham (4): Guildhall
Long Crendon (6): Courthouse
Long Melford (4): Melford Hall

Montacute (7a): Montacute House
Muchelney (8a): Priest's House
Nether Stowey (8a): Coleridge Cottage
Otham (1): Stoneacre
Rydal (14): Dora's Field, etc.
Selborne (2b): Selborne Hill
Selworthy (8a): village
Snowshill (7b): Snowshill Manor
Steventon (2c): Priory Cottages
Stoke-by-Nayland (4): *houses in Back Street*
Stoke-sub-Hamdon (7a): Priory
Stourton (7a): Stourhead
Styal (10b): village
Temple Sowerby (14): Manor House
Thorney (5): *Thorney Abbey House*
Tintinhull (7a): Tintinhull House
Troutbeck (14): Townend
West Wycombe (2c): West Wycombe Park, Church Hill and village
Wetheral (14): woods
Widecombe - in - the - Moor (8b): Church House
Winster (11a): Market House

The properties shown in *italics* are not actually owned by the National Trust, but are protected by covenants.

INDEX